Harry Watts
The Forgotten Hero

BY DAVID SIMPSON
AND RICHARD CALLAGHAN

Copyright © David Simpson and Richard Callaghan 2013

ISBN: **978 1 909486 01 0**

First Published 2013

My World
Chase House
Rainton Bridge Business Park
Tyne and Wear
DH4 5RA
Tel: 0191 3055165
www.myworld.co.uk

My World is an imprint of Business Education Publishers Limited.

British Cataloguing-on-Publications Data.

A catalogue record for this book is available from the British Library.

Cover design by **courage**, UK.

Printed and Bound in Great Britain by Martins the Printers Ltd.

Acknowledgements

A warm thank you goes out to everyone who has helped with this book.

Thanks firstly to Terry Deary for suggesting the book on Harry Watts, who despite our initial cynicism persuaded the authors that Harry was a man whose story needed to be remembered. Thanks to Sarah Stoner for her research and particularly her assistance in finding images for the book. Thanks to the staff of Sunderland City Library and to *The Sunderland Echo*. Thanks to Layla Ferdowsian at Courage Creative for her work on the design. Thanks also to Vicki Medhurst and Janet Robinson of Sunderland City Council and Jennie Lambert of Sunderland Museum and Winter Gardens for all their work in raising the profile of Harry Watts. A special thanks to the year 5 and 6 pupils at Grangetown Primary School: Lauren Petty, Matthew Brown, Tegan Burnip, Eleanor Brooke-Taylor, Niamh Alderson, Brandon Cheal, Alicia Crosbee and Leigha Faye McDonald for their endearing contributions to the book and thanks also to their head teacher Les McAnaney for encouraging their involvement. Finally we must give a special acknowledgment to Alfred Spencer the author of the *Life of Harry Watts; Sixty Years Sailor and Diver* published in 1911. Spencer died in February 1913 a little over two months before Harry's death in April of that year. Spencer's work remains the most valuable source of information about Harry and his life without which Watts would surely have remained forever the forgotten hero.

Foreword

BY TERRY DEARY

I confess. I'm a bit embarrassed. I thought I knew a little history … and especially the history of my home town, Sunderland. It seems our Irish Terrier knows more than I do. Embarrassing.

Back in 2011 I started writing a book about Victorian Railways and needed to check some facts on the Tay Bridge Disaster. There was an internet link to one of the divers who volunteered to recover the bodies. His name was Harry Watts. Now I like human interest stories, not statistics or dry facts, so I clicked on the link and began to read the diver's remarkable story. Then my eyes strayed to the biography details of Harry. I did a double take. It said simply "Born: Sunderland".

He was a hero. An amazing man with an inspirational story. Yet I had never heard of him. He was born half a mile from where I was born. I read more of the article and came across the ironic statement by the US philanthropist, Andrew Carnegie. 'You should never let the memory of this Sunderland man die.' And that's just what we have done, it seems.

When I realised the centenary of his death was 2013 I made it my mission to use the occasion to celebrate his life and bring him to the attention of the public. After all we all need heroes, people we can use as models we can aspire to.

My first port of call was the Sunderland Echo. I copied the internet article and sent it to the paper's heritage specialist,

Sarah Stoner. "Have you SEEN this story on the internet?" I wrote.

Sarah replied, "Yes. I wrote it."

Oh. Embarrassed again. At least Harry wasn't totally forgotten then. And so the campaign to commemorate Harry's daring deeds gathered pace.

It took a while to track down his burial place in Grangetown cemetery but at last I stood there in front of a weathered gravestone, his name almost as invisible as his memory. He's at peace now after a long and often painful life. But in that life he never complained or gave up. That's why we need a book to celebrate his life and achievements. We need stories of people like Harry Watts because they inspire us all to live our lives the best way we can ... and one of the best ways is to help others whenever we can.

The incredible story is now in your hands. Prepare to be fascinated, shocked, amused and informed. But above all be inspired. And tell everyone you know about him. Join the writers in making sure we never again let the memory of this Sunderland man die.

Contents

Introduction

Harry Watts was born in Sunderland in 1826. He lived through the reign of William IV, Victoria, and Edward VII, and died in Sunderland in 1913, at the age of 86. During his long and truly remarkable life he saved 36 people from drowning, married three times, lost three children, recovered bodies from the Tay Bridge and the Victoria Hall disasters, lost a finger in a diving accident, became a born-again Christian, a Temperance activist, a local celebrity, and had a biography commissioned in his honour. And then, in the turbulence of the Twentieth Century, he was forgotten.

April 23, 2013 marked the centenary of this extraordinary man's death. Although unknown by many, even in his home town of Sunderland, Harry's story is deserving of recognition, and his life worthy of remembrance. This book tells the story of Harry, his world, and the importance of remembering this forgotten hero.

The book also contains the contributions of eight students of Grangetown Primary School in Sunderland, less than a mile from Harry's final resting place. Taking episodes from Harry's tale, approached in their own inimitable style, they truly bring Harry's story to life, and we are delighted to include them in the book.

The Forgotten Hero

"I have today been introduced to a man who has, I think, the most ideal character of any man living on the face of the earth. I have shaken hands with a man who has saved thirty-six lives. Among the distinguished men whose names the Mayor has recited, you should never let the memory of this Sunderland man die. Compared with his acts, military glory sinks into nothing. The hero who kills men is the hero of barbarism; the hero of civilisation saves the lives of his fellows."

Andrew Carnegie, October 21, 1909, Sunderland.

Henry Watts was born on June 15, 1826 in Sunderland's Silver Street to William Watts, a mariner and Elizabeth Watts. He was born in the parish of Holy Trinity, named from the beautiful eighteenth century church of 1719 that still stands in Sunderland's East End today. It is one of the few remnants of Old Sunderland that Watts would recognise if he were around today.

Harry, as he was affectionately known to his family and friends, was the youngest of five children. The others in descending order of age were Isabella, William, Ellen and James all of whom grew up in the same impoverished circumstances.

Silver Street was situated in the East End or 'Old Sunderland' as it is sometimes known. It was a notoriously crowded and poor area of the town. Close to the eastern terminus of Sunderland's High Street and near the harbour, Silver Street was one of Sunderland's older streets. It was part of an area that had been a place of prosperity but increasingly came to be dominated by the poorer classes.

Like many streets in the neighbourhood, this street had been a home to many of the town's wealthier residents but over the decades, members of Sunderland's middle classes moved to the more serene environments of Bishopwearmouth at the western end of the High Street. One reason for the move was that the poor rate - a tax imposed to provide welfare for the poor - was much higher in Old Sunderland than it was in Bishopwearmouth.

Much of Old Sunderland was becoming a rough and ready part of town and had all the attributes of a typical early nineteenth century seaport. It was crowded, slum-infested and home to a legion of seedy riverside establishments frequented by drunken sailors. Throughout Harry's life this busy port continued to expand and as the town's population grew, overcrowding increased and the shipping lanes of the river mouth became ever busier.

Sunderland: an East End scene

When Harry was born George IV was on the throne but most of Harry's childhood spans the reign of this king's successor, William IV. When Harry was ten years old Queen Victoria ascended to the throne. Harry was one of those few people privileged enough to witness not just the entire Victorian age but the Edwardian age of Edward VII that succeeded it. Despite the trials and tribulations of a life in which family tragedy and serious illness darkened Harry's door he still lived to the grand age of 86, some three years into the reign of George V, the grandfather of our present queen.

Those 86 years saw some of the biggest changes the world had ever seen. It was an era of massive industrial expansion and enormous population growth and an era in which Sunderland played an important role. In the early part of Harry's life, the busy shipbuilding port of Sunderland was dominated by masses of wooden sailing ships crowding the harbour. By the later part of Harry's life these wooden vessels were superseded by iron steamships.

The sailing ships in Sunderland harbour must have been an impressive sight to see. When the winds gave favour to sailing, the view from the shores of Sunderland and other parts of the region was seemingly one of great beauty. All at once hundreds upon hundreds of ships would set sail, so that the entire seascape from the Tyne to Hartlepool was filled with a mass of elegant sails and masts.

By 1830 Sunderland was the most important shipbuilding centre in the country. There were 2,025 shipwrights working in Sunderland in 1850 and a further 2,000 working in related industries. It is well known that Sunderland was a shipbuilding town inhabited by shipbuilders but the huge number of sailors that inhabited the town is often overlooked. When it came to ships - and this may offer an explanation of a term used today - Sunderland was in the local dialect not just the home to those who would 'mackem' but also a major residence for those who would 'tackem' out to sea. Harry was a man who fell into the latter category.

Of course the ships built at Sunderland in the early part of Harry's life were entirely of wood, with some 150 constructed here in 1850. Iron ships were built at Sunderland from 1852 and by 1876 wooden shipbuilding had ceased in the town. It was a period of rapid change in Wearside's industrial landscape and a one that Harry Watts would witness firsthand.

Coal had been a major shipping export from Sunderland since the 1600s but the coal shipped through the town came from collieries further downstream around Fatfield and Washington. It wasn't until about the time of Harry's birth that deep coal mines started to open beneath the Magnesian Limestone that dominates the geological landscape around Sunderland. It brought further stimulation to the growth of the town. One significant event of this era was the opening of Monkwearmouth Colliery in 1835. By 1846 this colliery was the deepest mine in the country at 1,700 feet. It would remain in operation until its closure in June 1994 when it was the last remaining colliery in the Durham coalfield. Its site is now occupied by Sunderland's Stadium of Light.

Coal was brought to Sunderland's riverside on railways from deep east Durham pits like Hetton. At Sunderland it was loaded into legions of coal carrying ships berthed at staithes and drops along the River Wear such as Lambton Drops and Hetton Drops. These loading points were home to dangerous work and were sites at which Harry was often found working, particularly in his later career as a diver. The opening of Sunderland's docks was another important development in the shipping trade that Harry would have witnessed. These developments began with the opening of the woefully inadequate north dock in 1837 followed by the much larger south docks of the 1850s and 1860s. Again, these docks were familiar territory to Harry throughout his working life.

The industrial developments of the era brought growth and prosperity to Sunderland, but there was also a dark side. Overcrowding, poor sanitation and poverty were rife and life expectancy in the poor districts was low with many dying in their infancy.

Dating from 1719, Holy Trinity church in Old Sunderland would have been a familiar landmark to Harry Watts

Today, a relatively pleasant estate of modern houses occupies the site of Silver Street, the street of Harry's birth. The area bears little resemblance to the Old Sunderland of times past. Harry recalled that his family's abode encompassed little more than a tenement cellar and noted that it was frequently flooded by an overflowing drain.

In general, the Old Sunderland of 1826 was not a very healthy or pleasant place to live. It was littered with cesspits and piles of manure and although an act for cleansing, lighting and improving Sunderland was introduced in this year of Harry's birth, unhealthy conditions prevailed that created an ideal breeding ground for diseases like cholera.

In October 1831 when Harry was only five years old, Britain's biggest cholera epidemic swept the country killing more than 32,000 people. Sunderland played the rather ignomious role of being the port through which the disease entered the country after sweeping across Asia and Europe.

Many Sunderland lives, both young and old, were claimed by cholera. The first death in the country was a twelve year old girl called Isabella Hazard who lived near the River Wear but amongst the other early victims was Jack Crawford, a fifty six year old Sunderland resident best remembered as the hero of Camperdown.

For more than two centuries Jack Crawford has been regarded as the great hero of Sunderland. His renown has certainly overshadowed that of Watts and not always deservedly so. Crawford's fame dated back to 1797, when, in an act of extreme bravery - though some say a state of drunkenness - he nailed the fallen flag to the mast of the admiral's ship amidst heavy gunfire at the great naval battle of Camperdown. Crawford probably had no choice in the matter but was showered with bullets and shot through the cheek as he climbed the rigging. Amazingly, he lived to tell the tale. The nailing of the colours to the mast was a defiant statement of no surrender that immediately gained Crawford nationwide fame for this one heroic act.

Crawford was presented to the king following the battle victory. He was given a healthy government pension of £30 and presented with a silver medal by the people of Sunderland. Sadly, in his later days, he squandered the money and sold his medal. For Crawford, cholera only served to end a life of drunken poverty. Crawford, once the hero, was given an undignified burial in a pauper's grave. Harry Watts would be decorated with medals for a quite different kind of bravery and like Crawford, Harry would also lose his medals, but for very different reasons.

Jack Crawford, hero of Camperdown has overshadowed the heroics of Harry Watts

Like Watts, Crawford was a sailor, like Watts, Crawford was born into humble Sunderland origins and like Watts, it seemed for a time that Crawford's life would not receive a public memorial. However, in Crawford's case, the memories of his heroism eventually filtered their way back into Sunderland's public consciousness. In the late nineteenth century a rather romanticised interest in Crawford's heroism developed that seems to have been very noticeably absent in the later part of Crawford's life.

A campaign for a memorial in Crawford's honour in the later part of the century was partly inspired by the launch of a touring play by a Sunderland playwright. It was simply entitled *'Jack Crawford, the Hero of Camperdown'*. Public reaction was favourable. Crawford was no longer remembered as the drunk who had squandered his medal and his money. He was the hero once again. The ultimate result was the erection in 1888 of a commemorative headstone to Crawford in the cemetery at Holy Trinity church. It was followed in 1890 by the unveiling of a statue in Mowbray Park depicting Crawford in his heroic act.

Unlike Watts, whose list of heroic achievements stretches across a lifetime, Crawford's fame was based on that one single act of heroism, but it was an act that momentarily captured the hearts of the nation. Nevertheless it was almost a century before Crawford's achievement was properly commemorated in Sunderland. By contrast there is no statue to Harry Watts, even though a hundred years have passed since Harry's death.

Watts was a man who lived most of the later part of his life as a teetotal. He was a man who voluntarily saved the lives of scores of men and women, but in Sunderland his story is largely forgotten.

Memorial to Jack Crawford in Sunderland's Mowbray Park

Was the reluctance to commemorate Crawford and Watts somehow linked to their rough and humble origins? Certainly the delay in commemorating the lives of Crawford and Watts is in marked contrast to the story of Major General Sir Henry Havelock, another Sunderland 'hero'. His fame, like that of Crawford's is of doubtful renown, but for different reasons. Havelock's impressive statue can be seen in Mowbray Park only a short walk from Crawford's memorial but little time was wasted in commemorating this Sunderland military man.

Havelock, the son of a shipbuilder was born in 1795 in Bishopwearmouth and unlike Crawford or Watts was born into wealth and status. His statue stands on a plinth in Sunderland's pleasant park and another similar memorial to him can be seen in London's Trafalgar Square where he has Nelson and other esteemed notables for company. Street-names across Britain, as well as in Singapore, the USA,

Canada and New Zealand commemorate this Sunderland man. It was Havelock that rescued the garrisons of Cawnpore and Lucknow in India, in a conclusion to the horrific but ultimately preventable events of the Indian Mutiny of 1857. It was a mutiny that resulted largely from British insensitivity and imperial arrogance. It was at Lucknow in 1857 that Havelock died when he became inflicted with dysentery. Within only four years of his death Havelock's statue was placed in Mowbray Park.

By the time Havelock's memorial appeared in Mowbray Park, Harry Watts had already saved the lives of at least seventeen people, often at great risk to his own life, yet his humble acts of heroism were little known. Harry, the forgotten hero, had yet to even make the pages of the local newspapers. By the time Crawford's belated monument was unveiled in 1890 Harry had saved 35 lives and probably many more in his work assisting others.

* * *

The five year old Harry Watts and his family survived the cholera epidemic of 1831 that claimed the life of Crawford, but harder times and tragedy were never far away for the Watts family. Severe poverty in the household was compounded by the death of Harry's mother when Harry was seven and by the death of his father, William, when Harry was thirteen. William had been confined to bed with rheumatism for much of Harry's childhood. This was how Harry remembered his father. He could only recollect his dad going out to sea on one occasion in the days before the ailment had taken a serious hold.

Harry's eldest brother, also called William, had followed in the father's footsteps and sought a life at sea. Sadly, William junior drowned on board a ship *The Richard*, as it was thrown ashore in a gale at Tenby in Wales on August 3, 1844. William had made for the rigging in a desperate attempt to find safety. Unfortunately, a massive wave engulfed the ship and William was seen no more. The story of this tragedy would have made a great impression on the young Harry and may have shaped his instinct for saving people from the perils of the sea.

Harry was eighteen at the time of his brother's death, but despite his place as the youngest of the Watts children, responsibility had already fallen heavily on his shoulders. As a young boy Harry had, like many other Sunderland youngsters at this time, scraped coal dust from the beach and often waded into the sea to rescue flotsam and jetsam - pieces of wreckage and other items - from ill-fated ships in the hope of making ends meet. This would hardly provide an income for the family. Harry's brother, James, had also found work, at a baker's shop where wages included a provision for rations of the baker's ware that kept James well-fed but left him with only pennies to take home in pay.

Coal has often been gathered from the beach at Sunderland in times of hardship

James and Harry barely learned to read or write as children and in his later life Harry could write little more than his name. This lack of literacy was something that Harry regretted from time to time. It was a common problem amongst seafaring communities, a fact that Watts reflected upon when interviewed in his later years:

Aw wint ower ti' Hamburg yince, an' theere wes sivven on us aboard an' nut yen ov us cud read or write, nut even th' mate; didn't knaw ABC fra a gridiron, on'y th' skipper. Whin ony ships passed us, ef the cap'n was i' bed we hed to roust him oot ti read the nyams ov 'em. Yit, man alive, we made the passage awreet. An' here they are tiday, eddicated in Colleges an' High Skules, an' aw divn't knaw what, an', man, theers plenty ov 'em cuddent find theer way yam fra th' ferryboot lan'in' ef th' leets wes oot.

Harry's schooling consisted of little more than a weekly attendance at a Sunday School, where he was accompanied by James. It proved to be a painful experience for the two boys. Such was the poverty in the Watts family that the brothers attended without shoes and socks. Sunday School was traditionally a place where you wore your best clothes, so the Watts brothers were shunned by the other boys who refused to sit next to them.

The brothers stopped attending the school and might have been forgotten if it was not for the concerns of a teacher who enquired why they failed to attend. On learning the reason, the sympathetic teacher arranged for the two boys to be provided with suitable clothes. Each week, the clothes were collected on Sunday morning and returned the following day.

Whilst James was earning bread in a quite literal sense at the bakery, Harry started work at the age of nine with a more substantial wage. He would become the family breadwinner with earnings from his employment at Sunderland's Garrison Pottery. The pay amounted to one shilling and sixpence a week. The pottery, also known as The Sunderland Pottery, was one of a number in Sunderland at the time that utilised cheap local coal for working the kilns along with imported white clay and stone that often arrived as ballast onboard ships.

Pottery buildings, Sunderland

Established by the Dixon family around 1800 the Garrison Pottery occupied the site of an earlier pottery on Sandy Well Bank or Pottery Bank as it was later known. Harry's workplace was named from a neighbouring barracks or garrison dating from the 1790s. The barracks were bordered by the Black Cat Battery near Old Sunderland's Town Moor and were there to defend against naval attack. They had once been home to 1,528 infantrymen. Sadly, the barracks and the pottery site were lost during the development of Sunderland's Corporation Quay in the early 1930s.

Located near the harbour mouth, the Garrison Pottery was famous for its willow designs, frog-themed mugs along with illustrated jugs and other items that often featured Sunderland's bridge. The featured bridge was not the Wearmouth Bridge of today of course, but the earlier eighteenth century bridge of 1796. It had stood on the site of the present Wearmouth Bridge and was one of the best-known bridges in Britain, attracting admirers from all around the world. Throughout Harry Watts' lifetime it was the most famous landmark in Sunderland.

Examples of Sunderland Pottery showing the old Sunderland Bridge

The Garrison Pottery was only a stone's throw from Silver Street and although it is noted that as a boy Harry 'worked there for some time', he soon moved on to a new job in a weaving factory in Fitter's Row. This was situated in an area now occupied by the present day Rickaby Street and was Silver Street's neighbour. It lay just to the north east and for Harry it was yet another short walk to work. He remained working there until the age of thirteen. Unfortunately Harry's wage was not enough to satisfy the needs of a growing lad and his struggling family. Hungry and hardened to life, he made the decision to follow his late father and ill-fated brother and seek a life at sea.

A nineteenth century etching by Thomas Hemy of the old bridge at Sunderland

Harry Watts' bad luck

BY BRANDON CHEAL
Grangetown Primary School, Sunderland

Grangetown Young Writers

I don't know where to start, he had so much bad luck, from his terrible childhood to his dangerous adult life. Let me have a think. Harry Watts started his bad luck when he lived in a cellar, and he was not rich which didn't help him at all. Imagine swimming in your own house. He went to Sunday School but had no shoes and no proper clothes, just rags. He had no friends, just his older brother William. At the age of 14 he went off to sea for the first time, and while he was there he became a saviour (for the first time) and that was just a tester. When he came back it started, his father died. He heard as soon as he got back.

When he was 18 years old his eldest brother drowned and a sprout of luck came to his life when he got married, but he couldn't afford a honeymoon. He and his wife had 3 babies but they all died.

Losing his finger, swallowing sewage, losing his family, all sorts. I could officially say he had the worst luck ever.

Young Harry

BY TEGAN BURNIP
Grangetown Primary School, Sunderland
Grangetown Young Writers

When Harry Watts was younger, he was very poor. Harry was the youngest out of five children. He had two brothers called William and James. He also had two sisters called Isabella and Ellen. They lived in Silver Street in the east end of Sunderland. They lived in a cellar that was frequently flooded from a nearby drain. He lived with his mother and father. His mother was called Elizabeth and his father was called William. When Harry was seven his mother sadly died. She got very, very ill.

Life at Sea

"He stands five feet nine inches in height, weighs twelve and a-half stones, is straight as a pole, muscular and strong, and has a grip to the hand of him like a vice. Reddish hair and beard, what one may call a fresh-weather complexion, keen blue eyes which look out bold and fearless from under the overhanging brows; and to finish off with, a firm mouth, a determined jaw, and a big square chin. Alter his dress and place a winged helmet on his head, and you have a true specimen of the old Vikings those bold sea warriors who never knew defeat. There is no mistaking the fact that he is a son of Neptune, he has about him that alertness, that indescribable something which proclaims the fact."

Alfred Spencer, *Life of Harry Watts* 1911.

In June 1839, at the age of 14, Harry Watts went to sea. Motivated by the knowledge that the boys he knew who were apprenticed at sea had plenty to eat, Harry signed on to the *Lena*, a 299 ton brig, bound for Quebec. In signing on to the *Lena*, Harry agreed to a six year indenture which included clauses prohibiting him from attending "taverns or alehouses", and playing "dice, cards, tables, bowls, or any unlawful games". In return for which, and for Harry's "well and faithful" service, he received £48 over six years, the equivalent of £2,000 today. In addition, Harry bound himself to pay £100, twelve years wages, should he break the conditions of his contract.

From 1823 onwards, ships over 80 tons were required to carry apprentices like Harry. In 1835 new regulations were introduced to ensure that the rules were followed, meaning that masters were required to register the indentures with the local customs offices.

Harry went to sea at 14, leaving his father gravely ill. His father's parting words, "Good-bye Harry, I don't think I shall live to see thee any more. Be a good boy and serve your apprenticeship well," were prophetic as he was dead before Harry returned to Sunderland. His father's death at 53 left Harry's two sisters and his brother, James, homeless.

Life at sea for a 14 year old boy during the 1840s was by turns dangerous, exciting, repetitive, and incredibly boring. By all accounts the men on the *Lena* treated Harry well, being fully aware of his family's situation, but life was still very hard. Seamen were beset by a number of different ailments, illnesses and diseases, as well as the very real risk of accidental death.

Scurvy remained a significant cause of disease and death for sailors throughout the nineteenth century. Despite the fact that lack of fresh fruit and vegetables was understood to be a cause of the disease as early as James Cook's exploratory voyages to the South Seas a hundred years earlier, work to prevent the disease was patchy at best. It would be almost thirty years until the problem was directly addressed by government, with the 1867 Merchant Shipping Act making it mandatory for ships to carry stores of lemon and lime juice which was distributed to sailors and passengers in order to prevent scurvy.

A riverview of Sunderland in the early twentieth century

The *Lena* was built at the North Sands shipyard in Sunderland by James Leithead, who went on to take possession of it, and was the one who signed Harry's indenture that year. Launched in 1839, in all likelihood Harry was present on her maiden voyage. It was probably a "snow", a merchant ship rigged with square sails on two main masts, a very common type of merchant ship in the early part of the nineteenth century.

By 1840, the year after Harry Watts first went to sea in the

Shipbuilding at North Sands, Sunderland around 1880

Lena, there were 76 shipyards in Sunderland. In March 1814 there had been 23 yards in Sunderland. By 1815 this had risen to 31, and continued to grow almost exponentially. Between 1846 and 1854 Sunderland produced a third of the ships built in the United Kingdom, and by 1850 Sunderland was producing five times as many ships as it had in 1820.

When the *Lena* arrived in Quebec, Harry's shipmates went ashore and got drunk, and found themselves imprisoned. Harry and his fellow apprentice, the only two members of the crew not incarcerated, were given the task of taking the jailed men their dinners. It was while performing this duty that Nicholson, Harry's fellow apprentice, fell into the dock. The lad would have drowned had Harry not leapt into the water after him, saving his first life in the process.

After returning to England aboard the *Lena*, Harry set sail back to Canada on the *Cowen* under Captain Luckley.

Docking in Miramichi, New Brunswick, Luckley set off to buy a canoe. He was almost back at the ship when the canoe capsized, threatening to drown him. Luckily for Luckley, Harry Watts was waiting at the side of the ship for him, and seeing the captain struggling he grabbed a rope and jumped overboard, and rescued him.

* * *

Britain had gained control of Quebec in 1763, following the Treaty of Paris which ended the Seven Years War. The provinces which would go on to become Canada had been a battleground between Britain and America during the American War of Independence and the War of 1812, but by the time of Harry's voyages to Canada relations between Britain and the United States had normalised, the United States being far more concerned with the internal struggles which would lead, in 1861, to the American Civil War.

The Act of Union in 1840 saw Upper and Lower Canada abolished and united, creating the Province of Canada. The Act was passed in response to a report by John Lambton, the 1st Earl of Durham, who had been Member of Parliament for County Durham, Harry's MP, between 1812 and 1828. Lambton's report sought to identify the causes of the rebellions which had taken place in Upper and Lower Canada in 1837 and 1838. The rebellions had been driven, in no small part, by a desire for government which was responsible to the people of Canada. They were put down, with the ringleaders either executed or transported to the British penal colonies in Australia. The British government response was to send Lambton to Canada to propose reforms for appeasing the Canadian people, including the introduction of representative government in the colony.

Low Quay, the busy riverfront in Old Sunderland was the hub of Sunderland's quayside

* * *

From the *Cowen*, Harry went to the *James*, and by the time he was eighteen, he was aboard a ship called the *United Kingdom*. On a voyage from Quebec to Newcastle, carrying a cargo of Canadian timber, the *United Kingdom* found itself caught by storms in the Pentland Firth, in the north of Scotland. As the wind raged and the waves crashed against the ship, a boy named George Watson was thrown into the sea. So fierce was the storm that lowering a boat would have been impossible, and without the intervention of Harry, who grabbed up a rope and threw himself into the water after him, Watson would surely have drowned.

* * *

Timber was the most significant Canadian export during the nineteenth century, with British shipbuilding towns like Sunderland fuelling the demand. By 1840 Britain was importing nearly 500,000 loads of timber annually, up from just 15,000 in 1805. Many of the timber ships which took loads to Britain became passenger ships on the return journey, one timber ship capable of carrying over 200 people emigrating to the New World. Events such as the Great Famine in Ireland, stretching from 1845 to 1852, and the ongoing Highland Clearances in Scotland saw thousands of British people making their way across the Atlantic.

Mass emigration to Canada and the New World was very significant in the 1840s and 1850s

The British government, worried about losing their Irish population to the United States of America, attempted to attract the Irish to the British territories in Canada instead by controlling the prices of tickets to cross the Atlantic, restricting prices for crossings to just 15 shillings, as opposed to £4 or £5 for the trip to New York. The flow of Irish people into Canada continued throughout the decade, many finding jobs in the growing logging sector, chopping down the great northern forests to load onto ships like the *United Kingdom*.

● ● ●

In 1845, whilst aboard the *Protector*, docked at Woolwich, Harry saw a barge capsize and, acting with characteristic speed and resolve, saved the two men aboard it from drowning. By the age of 19, by his own actions, Harry had saved five lives.

During the middle part of the nineteenth century, when Harry first put to sea, life as a sailor remained an incredibly dangerous, unpleasant, and unrewarding one. The British Empire stretched across the globe, controlling territories on every continent, merchant seaman forming the lifeblood of this maritime trading empire. 1839, the same year that Harry went to sea, saw major power shifts across Britain's overseas interests.

In China, 20,000 chests of British controlled Indian opium had been seized and destroyed by Chinese forces, holding British Superintendant of Trade Charles Elliott and the British traders in China hostage, actions which would lead later that year to the commencement of the First Opium War. That war would see a decisive British victory, with fewer than 20,000 British troops defeating the entire Chinese empire, forcing the cessation of hostilities and the transfer of Hong Kong to British control with the Treaty of Nanking.

Just as tension mounted in China, British forces were marching into Afghanistan to begin the first Anglo-Afghan war, a disastrous campaign which would see just one of the 16,500 who departed India in 1839 make it back alive. The following year, as Harry travelled back and forth across the Atlantic, the Province of Canada was created by the 1840 Act of Union, uniting the territories of Upper and Lower Canada following the rebellions of 1837 and 1838.

Harry's life seems to have been unaffected by these great political changes, as was life for merchant seamen across the Empire. The British merchant navy was the largest in the world during this period, and it was growing very quickly indeed. Between 1839, (when Harry first put to sea) and 1850, the British merchant marine went from 21,670 ships to 25,984 ships, boosting the fleet by 994,000 tons. Shipbuilding technology had also moved on, with a shift from wooden ships to ships built using iron and steel, concentrating shipbuilding in towns close to areas of iron and coal production, one of the reasons why Sunderland's shipbuilding power continued to grow throughout the century.

The repeal of the Corn Laws by Robert Peel, leading to the adoption of Free Trade in 1846, saw the importance of the merchant navy increase massively. By taking away the protection which the Corn Laws had afforded to British landowners, Peel's reforms forced both prices and wages down, and meant that the British economy now became even more dependent upon the export trade to survive. And for exports, Britain needed merchant ships, merchant ships like the *Lena*, *Cowen*, *James* and the *United Kingdom*, and merchant seamen like Harry Watts. Between 1839 and 1844 British exports grew from £53m to £58m, about the same as a £220m growth in exports today.

As Britain's merchant navy grew in size and importance, the government took steps to improve conditions for the men so vital to its existence. The Merchant Shipping Act 1844 required every sailor leaving Britain to be registered and issued with a "ticket", so that the government knew exactly who was where and, crucially, which experienced sailors were available for conscription during times of war. The practice of "crimping", the kidnapping and press-ganging of sailors into service was common, with an Act for the Protection of Seamen Entering on board Merchant Vessels introduced in 1845. It aimed to stop the practice by licensing agents and imposing penalties for ships masters, captains or owners who used the practice to crew their ships. Examinations were introduced for officers and masters on merchant ships, although these wouldn't become compulsory until 1850.

Upon leaving the United Kingdom, Harry joined the *Protector*. In 1845, while the *Protector* was in port at Woolwich, Harry was working on the ship when he saw a barge full of sand capsize in the river, throwing the two men who were crewing her into the water. Harry jumped into the ship's boat and pulled the two men to safety, making them the fourth and fifth lives Harry had saved.

Married Life

"In the latter part of 1846, when he had just turned twenty and was only a few months out of his apprenticeship, Henry Watts married his first wife, Rebecca Smith, who was the same age as himself. Before the reader begins to denounce this early marriage as a foolish and improvident act, let him consider the circumstances of the case. Both these young people were orphans, and neither of them had a home. Therefore they could not be much worse off in any case, and as the chance of being better off for many years to come was extremely problematical, they decided to marry, their only fortune being youth and good health."

Alfred Spencer, *Life of Harry Watts* 1911.

In late 1846, a few months after completing his apprenticeship, Harry Watts married his first wife, Rebecca Smith. Both were twenty years of age. At the marriage service they were joined by other young couples who shared their big day. Once the ceremony was over they would, according to Harry, "aal gan hyam and get drunk", a state of affairs that Harry would look upon with some disdain in the later part of his life.

Harry and Rebecca were both orphans and previously homeless, so they pooled together what little resources they could to start their married life together. They moved into King's Entry just off Silver Street, the street where Harry was born. They owned very little. There was "scarcely a thing ti' put into it", Harry would note in a later recollection of his early matrimonial home.

Silver Street in Sunderland's East End was Harry's birthplace where Harry and Rebecca Watts set up home together

Of course, there was no honeymoon for the newly wedded Mr and Mrs Watts. The couple simply didn't have the resources to even consider such a thing.

Harry was soon off to sea again being "shipped before the mast" as it was known in the phrase of the time. The phrase "before the mast" signified the social position of the common seamen whose quarters lay within that part of the ship located before the mast. It marked the beginning of his post-apprenticeship career, and the beginning of his life as an adult sailor. This meant amongst other things that he was allowed to drink in the inns and taverns when he landed ashore.

It was not long before Harry, the fully-fledged sailor was back at sea and making rescues once again. In 1847 he was on board a ship called The *Express* under the command of a Captain Booth. While docked at Rotterdam six foreign seamen were working from a small boat attending to the ship which lay alongside when their lives were nearly brought to a tragic end. As their boat proceeded beneath an anchor hanging from the ship, the rope that held the anchor broke, smashing the boat beneath and leaving the men fighting for their lives. Harry's reaction was typical of the man. He leapt over the side of his ship and swam to their safety, skilfully rescuing all six. The rescues brought the number of lives saved by Harry into double figures, with eleven in total.

On return to Sunderland, Harry made the choice to remain ashore for a number of years, enabling him to spend more time with his new wife. Sadly, these were not always the happiest times for Harry. Though the details are scant, there were a series of tragedies for the couple in their attempts to start a family. Three children were born to Rebecca in the early years of the marriage but sadly none of the children seem to have survived their early infancy.

During his time ashore at Sunderland between 1847 and 1852 Harry's jobs included attending the rigging of ships in the harbour and working in other forms of employment associated with the quayside and river. He found work wherever he could and in a busy port like Sunderland there was always something to keep those who were strong and willing in work.

Although Harry's hopes of raising a family had been dashed - for now at least - his instinct for the saving of lives never left him in his time ashore. One Sunday afternoon in 1852 as Harry walked the South Pier he observed a crowd of spectators helplessly watching a young boy as he struggled for his life in the sea on the far side of the pier.

Seeing the plight of the boy, Harry wasted no time and jumped into the sea. It was a tiring rescue and Harry swam ashore, hauling the full weight of the boy and battling fiercely against the waves. The boy, called Paul, was in a state of exhaustion but was safe and well. He would not have survived the sea if it had not been for Watts.

With concern for the health of the young lad, Harry visited Paul's house in Flag Lane the following day to see how he was recovering from the ordeal. A rather large, sturdy-looking woman of a type quite typical to Sunderland's harbour community answered the door. Harry explained that he had rescued the boy the previous day and was calling to see how he was keeping. The woman was not at all impressed: "Oh, wey, that's nowt, canny man; he's bin owerboard mony a time!" she exclaimed, looking upon Watts with indignity and slamming the door in his face.

Paul was the first of two boys rescued by Watts in Sunderland that year. Later in 1852 Harry was working on board a ship called the *John Muller*. It was moored alongside Smurthwaite's Wharf when it was passed by a small boat operated by an elderly couple called Mattie and Jeanie Grey. Their work involved ferrying sandstone down the river from Hylton.

As Harry worked, a boy fell into the water. Watts was alerted to the emergency by the loud cry of "man overboard". Typically, Harry dived some twenty feet straight into the water falling so close to Mattie and Jeanie's boat that the splash drenched the furious couple.

Harry is threatened with a shovel while rescuing a boy

After Harry had brought the boy, who was still alive, to the surface he headed straight for the couple's boat to hand him over. "For goodness sake tak' haad o' the boy, aw's nearly duen!" Harry demanded of the couple. This failed to arouse the sympathy of the soaked Jeanie, a woman hardened to life on the river. She lifted her shovel to Harry and exclaimed, "Ye, Harry Watts! For two pins aw'd split thee skull wi' this shool! Thoo's fair drooned beyth me an' oor Mattie." Fortunately Jeanie realised Harry and the boy were in a troubled state of stress and exhaustion. She hauled them on board and took them ashore.

Later in his life, the rescued boy, named Matthew Maughan would save lives from drowning on numerous occasions in much the same way as Watts. In 1889, Maughan received a testimonial from the Royal Humane Society. The presentation took place at the Hartley Street Mission Hall in Sunderland and Harry Watts was amongst the speakers that day. Like

Watts, Maughan was a modest east end of Sunderland lad and it seems that Harry Watts' bravery had inspired Maughan in the performance of similar acts of courage.

It wasn't just accident prone boys for whom Harry came to the rescue. In 1853 Harry came to the aid of a young woman who had thrown herself into the sea at Hendon and was determined to end her life within its depths. Harry, so often in the right place at the right time, swam out to thwart this attempted suicide and brought the woman safely back to dry land. As she regained consciousness she protested to Harry, "Oh let me be in, let me be in", at least according to a rather melodramatic account by Harry's biographer, Alfred Spencer.

An early photograph showing a river view at Sunderland

Harry refused: "I've had ower much trouble ti' get thi oot!" he explained. The woman was taken into custody by a river policeman called Nixon Donkin and charged the next day with attempted suicide. Harry had to give evidence, as suicide was considered a crime. Eventually, though, the woman was released.

Watts would be responsible for saving a further two lives in 1853. In one incident he rescued a girl who had fallen into a canal at the port of Cardiff where he was docked at the time and in another he pulled a trimmer called William Smith to safety after he had fallen into Sunderland dock. Trimmers were involved in keeping even levels of coal on board collier ships as they were loaded with coal. It was a critical job as it was essential for preventing ships from listing. It could also be dangerous as the ships were loaded with the coal from chutes at speed. The trimmers on board had to work frantically with their shovels to keep the load safe.

Victorian photograph showing the Thames at Wapping

So far Harry had survived his rescues unscathed and in good health. That was about to change. During 1854 cholera was sweeping the country once again. There was no generally accepted understanding of its causes, it was mostly thought to be airborne and few accepted that it was linked with sewage, sanitation and contaminated drinking water. This was despite the work of the Yorkshire-born physician John Snow, who had thoroughly researched its causes and had very clear evidence of the link. The sanitary situation in London was particularly horrendous at the time. Much of the capital's sewage was discharged straight into the River Thames making it a lethal health risk for anyone who had the misfortune to end up in its waters. The river was described as being of a yellow-brown colour and having the consistency of soup. The river at Wapping in the eastern part of London was very likely one of the most badly contaminated sections of the Thames.

It was in the summer of 1854 that Harry Watts and a fellow sailor were walking along the dock side at Wapping when that familiar scream of "man overboard" was heard. This was the usual trigger to spring Harry Watts to the rescue. The boy had gone under and even in the cleanest of waters this was a sure sign of danger. Harry skilfully and instinctively observed the location of the child's head and hand as he disappeared beneath the murky Thames. Harry urgently removed his coat and prepared to jump into the water from the bridge that crossed the dock.

Harry was unable to remove his sailor's coat quickly enough and it caught on his sleeve. There was no time to waste and as he dived into the lethal Thames water he unwillingly dragged the coat with him. As he plummeted into the depths of this open sewer nothing could be seen within its grim, unpleasant soupy darkness. It was only by Watts feeling his way in the waters with an urgent sense of touch that he was able to find the boy, grip him tightly and bring him to the surface.

With Harry and the boy safely ashore on the river bank, a mysterious, unidentified man, only described in Harry's memory as a "gold-braided official" approached Harry to praise him for what he called "a noble deed". He asked Harry where he hailed from. Harry told him that he was from Sunderland. The man said "Sunderland should be proud of him" and casually remarked that if ever Harry should come to London again he should call at his house and that he would not go unrewarded. He gave Harry his address.

Harry does not seem to have recalled or asked who this mysterious gentleman was. It did not occur to him to do so and it was not in his nature to accept reward, but he thanked the gentleman and retained the address as he headed back to his ship to change his clothes.

During the rescue Harry had consumed enough contaminated Thames water to leave this toughened mariner seriously ill. He took ill on board the ship and on return to Sunderland was attended by a doctor. For weeks Harry was confined to bed and nursed by his wife as he fought with the

Nineteenth century view of Wapping Warf

illness that left him unable to work. The sickness would stay with him for three months. Watts' situation made life all the more difficult for the struggling couple.

It seems that Harry's three little children were still alive at this time and his inability to work pushed the family to breaking point. Harry's illness had left him worn and frail, a shadow of his usual, healthy self. He was soon barely recognizable and was no longer the sturdy Sunderland seaman that everybody knew. Harry's condition and recovery could not have been made any better when combined with the worrying challenge of providing for his helpless family. Necessity forced him to recall the words of the gentleman that he had met in London, the man who had made that kind offer of reward. Harry had barely begun to recover when he invested all the strength he could muster to leave his bed and make his way to the dockside to board a ship bound for the Thames.

On reaching the Thames, the ship docked at the Long Reach near Gravesend several miles from London to sell its cargo, forcing Harry to request the loan of three shillings to go and search out the gentleman. Sadly it was all in vain. When, after some considerable effort, Harry located the gentleman's abode and had explained who he was and why he had come, Harry's humble request to receive the reward was refused. "We cannot believe every tale that is told us", Harry was told and it was even suggested that Harry could be an impostor. "We have impostors coming here every day, and how am I to know

A nineteenth century view of the Thames at Long Reach

but who you are". If this were the same gentleman who had promised Harry the reward, then the reason for his change of heart is not known. Perhaps he simply did not recognize Harry. Whatever the reason for not receiving reward, the despondent Harry returned to his ship.

Fortunately Harry's health began to return and he was soon working at sea once more. Sadly it may have been too late for his family. The details are vague but it seems Harry's three young children died at some stage during this unhappy period and what is more, further tragedy would follow.

. . .

On three occasions during Harry's life, all between 1856 and his retirement in 1861 Harry, the sailor found himself shipwrecked. The second occasion involved the shipwreck of *Elizabeth Jane*, a ship that belonged to Mr Thompson, a Sunderland draper and the third involved another Sunderland ship called *Balmoral Castle*. Both of these shipwrecks occurred off the coast of East Anglia, one in heavy seas near Yarmouth and the other in a gale near Lowestoft. On both occasions Harry and the crew were brought to safety.

Similarly on the first occasion that Harry suffered shipwreck he was once again rescued, but this time much closer to home. Sadly, however it was this rescue that resulted in tragic personal consequences for Harry. Around 1856 Harry was returning to Sunderland from London on board a ship called the *John Murray* in a heavy storm. The ship struggled to enter Sunderland harbour and as it turned, the cargo shifted and caused the ship to run aground near the south pier where crowds were watching.

Harry's wife Rebecca helped in the launching of a lifeboat from the shore which went to the rescue of the crew. Catching site of her husband on board the rescue boat, Rebecca waded into the sea up to her waist to greet him. This brief and happy reunion would ultimately result in a tragic end for the couple. Rebecca's exposure to the wet and cold brought about a sickness that resulted in consumption and in her death within a short matter of time.

There was now only one Watts family survivor to keep Harry company, a little 'fancy dog' that had belonged to Rebecca. The dog's name and breed is not recorded but it would join Harry on his next journey beyond the shore. It too would nearly see its fate sealed by the sea. Late in 1856 as Harry worked on board a brig called the *Susannah* off the coast of Great Yarmouth the dog fell overboard. The sails were set for full ahead and the crew grumbled at the request to turn the ship around. Harry told them that it was no problem and that he would rescue the dog himself, jumping quickly into the water. The crew then turned the ship to rescue the exhausted Harry clutching the very lucky, surviving dog.

A letter to a mother

BY ALICIA CROSBEE
Grangetown Primary School, Sunderland

Grangetown Young Writers

To Paul's Mum,

Yesterday my friend Harry rescued your son, but this morning he went to see if he was ok. He knocked on your door and you answered, he explained what happened and you said, "Oh. wey that's nowt man; he's bin owerboard many a time" then slammed the door in his face. I'm not impressed, I want you to go and apologise to Harry for that rudeness.

Yours sincerely,

Elizabeth Watson.

A rescue of a dog

BY LEIGHA-FAYE MCDONALD
Grangetown Primary School, Sunderland
Grangetown Young Writers

Harry Watts and his wife had a little dog called Spotty. Harry looked after Spotty after his wife died. Harry and Spotty went on a massive ship. The ship was called Susannah. Near Great Yarmouth it was stormy and rainy. While everyone was rushing into the cabin, Spotty fell overboard! The skipper ordered for the ship to be turned around to save Spotty. Everyone grumbled and thought that it was a waste of time to save the little dog.

Harry got very angry and jumped into the sea. The skipper cared very much and got a rubber ring and threw it in. The waves were crashing and Harry finally got the rubber ring. Harry shouted up "pull the ring!" When he got on board and went down to the cabin he got a towel and dried himself and Spotty. He thanked the skipper for turning the ship around. Harry loved Spotty, and loved his wife.

Swallowing sewage

BY LAUREN LOUISE PETTY
Grangetown Primary School, Sunderland

Grangetown Young Writers

Harry Watts was kind and a hero. He saved many people, but once he swallowed some sewage, and here is the horrible tragic story.

In 1854 Harry was walking around the dock side at Wapping, London. The river was a yellow brown colour with the texture of soup, and full of people's excretions. Suddenly a loud fearful cry for help appeared out of the disgusting sea, and Harry looked to see a boy overboard. Harry just could not stand and watch the boy drown. Harry jumped in and dived to save him but time was ticking, and he could not remove his sailor coat fast enough. The boy started to sink and Harry could not find him, so he reached out and tried to find the boy. Finally he found the boy and brought him up to shore. A man who seemed to be of great importance congratulated Harry on saving the boy and becoming a hero, and promised him a reward.

Unfortunately Harry had swallowed some sewage which made him so seriously ill that he could not work and his family became very poor. So when Harry recovered he went and found a ship bound to London, and tried to find the man who promised the reward. Harry had to borrow money to make the trip but when Harry finally found the man he had forgotten Harry, and put him down as an impostor. So Harry never collected his award but did save the boy.

Finding Faith

"He is of the old-fashioned type of Christian. He knows nothing and cares nothing about religious controversy ; his simple faith in the main doctrines of Christianity is all-sufficient for him, and, it may be said, is a great and increasing comfort to him in his declining years. He is an optimist to his finger tips, always bright and cheerful; and he is so earnest and vigorous even now in his eighty-fifth year, that it is good to be in his company for a while. One scarcely knows to whom to liken him so far as his religious life is concerned."

Alfred Spencer, *Life of Harry Watts* 1911.

By the age of 31, Harry Watts was an experienced seaman, a man recently widowed, living in the house of his sister and her children, and when at home in Sunderland he was known to enjoy a drink. New Years Day 1857 was to change Harry's life forever. Brought back to his sister's house by four women, Harry had consumed so much alcohol his sister feared for his life. Waking in the early hours of the morning, Harry was seized by a feeling of pure dread, and claimed to have seen a huge black cloud, and heard a voice say, "Choose this day whom ye will serve".

Even in a life filled with colourful incidents, divine intervention must rank among the most colourful, and it certainly seems to have had a startling effect on Harry's life. Upon hearing the voice, he leapt from his bed and shouted to his sister, "Bella! Bring me the Bible!" Kneeling, he prayed to God, asking him to pardon his sins. It really was a Damascene moment in Harry's life, for from that day forward he would never again touch a drop of drink.

Harry became heavily involved in the church, first with the mission of a Mr Thomas Hanson of Coronation Street, and then with the Primitive Methodists at the Flag Lane Chapel. Primitive Methodism was a sect of Methodism which had been established around 1810 by Hugh Bourne and William Clowes. By the time of Harry's conversion in 1857, Primitive Methodism had become a significant religious force in Sunderland. The Flag Lane Chapel had opened on September 3, 1824, funded entirely by the subscriptions of the congregation. Sunderland was a hotbed of Primitive Methodism, with many of the most noted preachers making their way to the town to speak.

Sunderland was so significant to Primitive Methodism

that in 1868 the Sunderland Theological Institution was opened for the training of Primitive Methodist ministers. Sunderland hosted the Methodist Conference on numerous occasions during Harry's life, 1833, 1849, 1868 and 1890. From Sunderland, the Primitive Methodists spread out across the North East, with chapels established across the region, particularly in what became classified as the Sunderland Circuit. The Primitive Methodists organised their church into 72 Circuits, with the circuits grouped into 4 Districts, Tunstall in Staffordshire, Nottingham, Hull and Sunderland.

Membership grew over the period too, from 920 in the early 1840s to 1,623 in 1850 and 1,979 in 1860. By 1908, the Sunderland Circuit of the Primitive Methodists could boast almost £31,000 in property, equivalent to £1.7m today, and a quarterly income of £240 2s 10d (£13,000). During Watts' time they had spread throughout the Durham coalfield, sent ministers to preach in Northumberland, and preached open air sermons to congregations of thousands.

In that context then it is perhaps not surprising that Harry should attach himself to the Primitive Methodists, the position of his hometown in their congregation being so significant. The transformation in Harry's life, however, remains truly remarkable. Not only did Harry become a devout Christian, but an active campaigner for the Temperance movement.

Drinking and drunkenness were growing concerns in Sunderland during Harry's life, with many fearing the negative effect that alcohol consumption had on their society. The Sunderland Temperance Society had been founded in 1830 to attempt to stem this growing tide, and had become a significant force in the town. Considering Harry's personal history, however, it is remarkable the extent to which he became involved in the movement. Here was a man who had no education apart from that afforded him by a life of hard work on the sea, yet he regularly spoke at public meetings advocating temperance, preached and evangelised to those he met, and clearly regarded temperance and his religion as the cornerstones of his life.

St Peter's church, Monkwearmouth

Although the popular impression of Victorian temperance is that of a movement dominated by the middle classes, Harry was not alone as a working class campaigner. Indeed, a temperance faction had grown alongside the Chartist movement for universal suffrage which developed from the publication of the People's Charter in 1838. Chartist leaders hoped that a commitment to abstinence would lend their movement an air of respectability which would in turn persuade political leaders to take them seriously. Unfortunately for the Chartists, political leaders took them very seriously indeed, moving to crush Chartism just ten years later in 1848.

The Chartists may have failed, but the groundswell of working class activism which had occasioned its rise was still evident in areas of society which posed a lesser threat to the establishment, including the temperance movement. Throughout the 1850s and '60s there were numerous bills to limit or totally prohibit the sale of alcohol introduced into Parliament, none of which made it into law. In 1853 the sale of alcohol in Scotland was regulated by the Forbes Mackenzie Act, which saw pubs closed at 11pm on weekdays and all day on Sundays, and between 1853 and 1860 the tax on spirits in Scotland more than doubled as politicians sought to address the problem of working class alcoholism.

It was merely six months after his conversion that Harry married his second wife, Sarah Ann Thompson. They were married at the parish church of St Peter's Monkwearmouth on June 7, 1857, listing Dock Street, Monkwearmouth as their place of residence. In fact they lived in the east end of Sunderland, but moved to Dock Street just long enough so they could be married at St Peter's. They shared twenty seven years of marriage, with Sarah Ann passing away in 1884.

Sarah Ann was born in 1838, and married Harry at age 19. Her father, Edward, had been a river pilot. Upon their marriage, Harry and Sarah moved in with Harry's mother-in-law, Martha Thompson, and they are recorded on the 1861 census as living together in Martha's house at 3 Metcalfe Yard, with Martha, Sarah's 12 year old sister Frances, and Harry and Sarah's son Thomas.

Martha went missing in mysterious circumstances. She was at the fish market one day, probably the one sited at Ettrick's

A gathering of River Wear pilots in the 1890s. Harry Watts would have known these men well. Harry's second wife, Sarah was the daughter of a river pilot

Quay, on the South side of the river which was cleared in the 1930s to allow for the construction of Corporation Quay. She is said to have disappeared, never to be seen again, although her shopping basket was later discovered in the river by the ferryboat man. Upon Martha's death Sarah became a woman of some means, inheriting five or six of the houses in Monkey's Yard, along with some other property.

When called to the solicitor's office to sign the deeds for the property, Harry took so much time to sign the forms that the solicitor, Mr Snowball, lost patience with him and said, "Come along man; you're going to use up all the ink in the office. Anyone might think you were signing a Royal Charter", to which Harry replied, "Aye, aye, Mr Snowbaal; be canny wiv us; ad's deem' me best."

Sarah and Harry had six children, Martha, Sarah Frances, Thomas, Lydia, Alfred, and a second child called Sarah

Frances, born in 1884 following the death of the first. Thomas grew up to become Harry's assistant, and later followed in his footsteps as a diver.

Harry remained committed to temperance for the rest of his life, taking any opportunity offered him to try to convert people to his cause. A demonstration of just this tendency came when, as working for the River Wear Commissioners as a diver, he was sent to do a rather unusual job. During a period of heavy rain the drains near Rutland Street in Millfield had become blocked, with flood waters rising to a height of sixteen feet. Harry was dispatched to clear the blockage, which was made up in no small part of dead cats and dogs, as well as rubbish of various kinds.

The sight of Harry at work was so unusual that a large crowd had gathered around by the time he was finished. Coming up out of the water, Harry saw the audience he'd garnered, removed his helmet, and gave them an impromptu speech on the subject of temperance.

A nineteenth century view of Sunderland High Street

In 1873 Harry witnessed a brewer's horse and dray, carrying casks of ale, fall from the Wear ferry into the river. The horse was very valuable and Squire Anthony Ettrick, with whom Harry was talking at the time, said that he'd give a great deal to see the horse saved, as it was very valuable. Harry said he'd save it, but on one condition, that he was allowed to throw the cargo into the river.

The squire quickly agreed and Harry leapt into the water after the horse, unfastening the dray and pushing the barrels of ale into the river, mounting the horse and riding it, with some difficulty, to the safety of the riverbank. Having both saved a life and rid the world of some not inconsiderable amount of alcohol, Harry must have been quite pleased with himself. Unfortunately, when pushing the barrels into the river he had made the mistake of leaving the bungs in the barrels, preserving the beer for the people of Hylton where the barrels washed ashore some time later.

Harry's rescue of the brewer's horse in 1873

Harry the Diver

"A set of ordinary diving apparatus consists essentially of seven parts, viz., (a) a helmet with corselet ; (b) a waterproof diving dress ; (c) a length of flexible tube with metal couplings ; (d) pair of weighted boots ; (e) pair of lead weights for breast and back ; (f) a life line ; (g) an air pump."

A Diving Manual : Submarine Appliances and their uses by R. H. Davies 1909.

From August 19, to November 19, 1861, Harry Watts, now 35, served on board the brig *Martha* of Sunderland. It was Harry's last voyage as a mariner, a career in which he had been employed since the age of fourteen. It would by no means mark the end of Harry's adventures and was merely the beginning of a new chapter in his life that would feature a whole new series of heroic acts.

Following his discharge from *Martha*, Harry found himself employed as a diver for the River Wear Commissioners, a career in which he would be employed for the rest of his working life. The dates are uncertain but it seems he commenced the work in the early part of 1862.

Harry was well-suited to diving. He was after all a powerful and accomplished swimmer and was fearless of the watery depths. These were not the only factors. Harry's sobriety, his physical strength and his common sense were all desired attributes. This was coupled with his ability to stay calm under pressure and in diving, working under pressure is a quite literal requirement. Harry's combined qualities suggest that diving was his natural vocation. In short, he was destined to become a diver.

Harry Watts' new employers were the River Wear Commissioners (RWC) who had played an important role in the growth of Sunderland as a port. Established in 1717, the Commissioners were set up to improve and maintain Sunderland's harbour, ensuring that the river remained safe and navigable for ships at all times. Such work was of immense commercial importance for Sunderland as it encouraged trade and ensured the growth of Sunderland as a port. Over the decades the RWC built piers, lighthouses, docks, warehouses, quays and facilities for loading and discharging ships.

The Lighthouse and old south pier at Sunderland were built by the River Wear Commissioners

The RWC removed the enormous sandbanks that were a major obstacle for shipping and dredged the river, increasing its depth and widening its course. In addition, during the second part of the eighteenth century, they built piers protruding into the sea as breakwaters on the north and south side of the river mouth. These were all measures to improve the river's navigation and those piers would be supplemented later by much longer structures, namely the Roker Pier built

1885-1903 and the New South Pier constructed from 1893 to 1912.

Ballast carried by ships for maintaining buoyancy had proved to be a long standing problem for Sunderland's harbour and this was one of the issues the Commissioners tackled head on. When ships arrived at Sunderland to pick up their cargo, the ballast they had been carrying had to go somewhere. Much of it was dumped on the shore, indeed several coastal areas of Sunderland are actually built on its foundations. The problem was that much of the ballast - it was comprised of stone, flint and sand from London and other parts of England - ended up in the River Wear. Removing the ballast was a job for a diver.

The Old South Pier in Sunderland harbour

During his period of training for the new job, Harry was placed under the tuition of a West Country diver employed by the RWC. There seems to have been an attempt by this mentor to frighten Harry with stories about the deaths that often came to divers as they set about their work and these deaths were described in morbid detail. The West Country man also played tricks on Harry while they were underwater, perhaps to undermine Harry's confidence or possibly test his nerve. In truth the man's motives for telling such stories and playing the tricks are unknown. Harry's biographer, Alfred Spencer suggested the man was jealous of Harry in some way, but maybe it was a genuine attempt to warn Harry about the perils of diving and ensure he was suited to the job. If so, he needn't have worried, the dangers facing divers were certainly very real, but Harry was not a man who could be frightened easily.

One of the first incidents in which the now fully-trained Harry was exposed to serious danger came around 1864 while he was repairing a sluice gate at Sunderland's docks. Harry became entangled in some rope which he was using to carry out his work. The yarn caught around the sluice and the collar of Harry's diving helmet. He couldn't signal to be drawn to the surface as he was stuck, but managed to keep calm. With as great an effort as he could muster he propelled himself backward with substantial force. This released him from the entanglement but broke a stud on his collar exposing him to sudden pressure and breathlessness. Fortunately, he returned safely to the surface.

There would be many other incidents of danger. On one occasion Harry recalled being trapped in a thick bed of seaweed while attempting to recover newly patented paddles from a tugboat belonging to a Mr Scott that had been shipwrecked in the Farne Islands. On another occasion in Sunderland harbour Harry was applying concrete underwater when he was thrown into danger by the accidental simultaneous explosions of several shots that resulted from nearby blasting operations.

Harry Watts in his diving gear

Harry was certain that he had narrowly escaped death in this particular incident, but in the event only one of his fingers was broken. He was, however, tipped upside down by the blast, a dangerous position for a diver to be in as we will soon discover, but Harry was hauled out by his assistants, feet first.

Early recorded diving work in which Harry was involved included blasting rocks beneath the Wear below Lambton Drops (near the old Wearmouth Bridge) in about 1864 and removing around 400 tons of stones from inside the old pier at the mouth of the river about 1870.

Harry's work in and around the river mouth meant he was often in the right place at the right time when people were in need of rescue. The first rescue during Harry's time as a diver took place near Sunderland's South Outlet in 1862 when a boat containing two boys capsized in severe weather. As usual Harry was straight to their rescue. He jumped into the water still wearing one of his heavy weighted diving boots which caused him to get cramp. This cannot have made the rescue easy but he held onto the boys until a coble boat arrived at the scene. Harry and the boys boarded the boat and returned to the river bank.

The following year Harry came to the rescue of children

Coal drops near Wearmouth bridge pictured around the 1840s

again, this time at Panns Ferry where a boy and girl were playing on timber tied up alongside the bank of the Wear. A powerful ebb tide, not expected by the children, swept the youngsters down the river at speed. Harry who was in the engine house of a neighbouring steam crane spotted them, dived in and swam to their rescue. It proved to be a challenging effort, but again, Harry brought them safely ashore.

Harry's next rescue was three years later in 1866 and was remarkable for being the very first Harry Watts' rescue to be reported by a newspaper. The report detailed the saving of the life of the sixteen year old son of an engineer employed on one of the RWC dredgers. The lad, named Smith, who was on board the dredger, accidentally fell overboard while it was berthed in a new Graving Dock (a dry dock) that was full of water at the time. Watts jumped in, brought the lad to safety and the exhausted young man was revived.

The reporter commented: *"This is the twenty-second time that Watts has so nobly exerted himself in saving persons who have been in imminent danger of being drowned"*. At twenty-two rescues, it was a wonder the press had taken so long to catch up with Harry's life saving heroics.

While each of Harry's rescues is on record, it is likely that many personal escapes solely involving Harry have gone unrecorded, though some moments of note were later recalled by Harry himself.

In one incident in 1870 as Harry was removing stones in the river mouth from inside the old pier he came face to face with a hideous Devil Fish, its mouth wide open and poised to attack. With only a knife for defence Harry signalled to be brought to the surface where he collected a boathook and then returned underwater. The fish was still there. In the words of Alfred Spencer, he

> *"rammed the head of the boathook into its mouth and so held it to the ground till he dispatched it with his knife."*

The actual danger and threat that Harry faced in this incident was perhaps exaggerated by Spencer, who seemed determined to elevate Watts' to saintly piety. For Spencer, a fight with a Devil Fish possibly took on a certain Christian symbolism.

This wasn't the only time Harry faced danger from a creature of the depth. In one undated incident, while working in the Wear beneath Hetton Drops, he felt something exert a fierce grip on his arm. Fearing that his diving gear would be pierced he signalled to be brought to the surface. Spencer records that Harry compared the grip to that of "Satan's own sel". This time, the foe turned out not to be a Devil Fish or

Nineteenth century view of Sunderland showing the bridge from the west

even the devil himself, but a twenty inch crab covered with spiny needles that had taken Harry firmly in the grip of its claws.

The threat posed by crabs and fish was one thing but there was also real danger of being crushed, injured or trapped. This was a particular concern for a diver working in a busy river mouth. Close escapes of this nature recorded by Harry included in one incident, the collapse of a large retaining riverside wall as Harry worked underwater. Harry described the event where pieces of stone fell on his feet followed by a "noise like thunder" that alerted him to danger. He signalled a request to be brought to the surface and was brought safely aboard a lighter as the whole quay wall, a quite substantial structure, plummeted into the river. It would almost certainly have buried Harry alive had he not responded to the danger so quickly.

It is hard to imagine anything worse than being trapped underwater by a falling wall, except perhaps being trapped by a sinking ship. This happened to Harry on one occasion when a steamer that had been wrecked and damaged on the rocks was brought into Sunderland's South Dock for assessment. Harry was sent underwater to inspect the damage when suddenly the heavy vessel listed to the side pinning Harry down. Fortunately for Watts the ship had pinned him into three to four feet of mud. He signalled to his assistants above to pull him up and with their help found his way out, in Spencer's words by

scratching and scrambling his way through the horrible mud till he got clear of the ship and so came to the surface, after a most exhausting trial of his strength and endurance.

In 1866 and 1867 further rescues of boys were made by Harry – and it nearly always seemed to be boys. This isn't surprising since many boys were employed in dockside labour and their inexperience made them accident prone. The first

Lambton and Hetton Staithes, Sunderland pictured around 1910

incident in September 1866 involved a lad called William Hall who fell overboard the RWC quay and the second involved a boy who fell off the Custom House Quay to become number twenty-four in Harry's increasingly impressive list of rescues.

For his twenty-fifth rescue in 1868, Watts made the local newspaper again though the rather short news report recording the incident suggests Watts was still not widely known:

Twenty-five Lives Saved by One Individual.

In the employ of the Wear Commissioners is a man named Henry Watts, who has a perfect penchant for rescuing lives, and has in one way or another succeeded in saving twenty-five individuals. The twenty-fifth case was on Friday night, when, about seven o'clock, a boy named John Fox, living in Mill Street, fell out of a boat at the Mark Quay into the river. Watts was at no great distance, and immediately he heard a lad was overboard he jumped into the river, and with some difficulty grasped the lad and brought him ashore.

The summer of 1869 saw the rescue of yet another boy by Harry and then in the following year Harry was involved in a rescue that could have been particularly disastrous had he not been so close at hand. The incident in question took place on June 7, 1870 when eleven people consisting of three adults and eight children took a pleasure cruise up the River Wear on board a gig called the *White Lily*. It was a trip undertaken merely for pleasure on what was presumably a pleasant summer day. The passengers included a boat builder by the name of Mr Friend Lamb accompanied by his wife and five children who were aged from two to ten years. Mr Lamb's cashier, called Hartley French, was also on board with three of his children.

Old postcard of the early twentieth century depicting the River Wear and its banks

At a point close to a spot called Burde's Lime Kilns the oars of the *White Lily* seem to have come into contact with a paddle steamer called *Wansbeck* that was coming down river. The clash caused the *White Lily* to capsize throwing all its passengers into the river. It was fortunate that Harry was on his way up river at the time where he was going to attend to some work. Harry, assisted by others, swam to the rescue of the party and brought them to safety by placing them on board the steam tug. It was soon realised that two of the children were missing. Instinctively, Harry swam to the overturned gig and found two little children clutching for their lives within it. Harry brought them to safety.

Always modest, Harry only claimed credit for rescuing one of the eleven passengers that day, but the facts reported at the time suggest he was responsible for saving the majority. Harry saw that the two families were deployed safely ashore before returning to the keel in which he was working with a companion called Robert Wilson. "Hurry up, now, we shall have to make up for lost time", Harry instructed Wilson. In the course of events that day it may be that this hasty desire to complete the work on schedule caused Wilson to fall overboard near Hetton Drops. Harry, once again dived in to the rescue, this time to save his working companion. It was certainly a busy day for Harry.

At a much later date, in a letter posted in September, 1875 Wilson would express his gratitude to Harry giving thanks to

*...our respected townsman, Mr Harry Watts, for the heroic
manner in which he saved me from drowning on the 7th June,
1870, while employed on the River Wear near Hetton Drops
when I accidentally fell overboard in about 24 feet of water.
Mr Watts sprang from a vessel lying near into water and rescued me from my perilous position.*

The year 1870 certainly proved to be an eventful year for
Harry, with a further rescue taking place later that year of a
boy who had fallen into the Wear near the Tide Jetty. More life
saving River Wear rescues followed throughout the decade
and again it always seems to have been boys. The rescues
included a lad called Edward Bolton saved by Harry in
1875, two boys, James Taylor and Henry Dobson, rescued in
separate incidents in 1876 and a man named John Lonsdale.

As a diver, Harry's work was not solely confined to work
within the river. In and around Sunderland and east Durham
there were many coal mines that flooded with considerable
loss of money to the mine owners. Such floods were often
caused by the failure of pumps. There are several letters of
praise from colliery owning companies that acknowledged
Harry Watts' part in rescuing their mines by fixing pumps
or clearing the pumping equipment of debris. There are
acknowledgements of Harry's work at Wheatley Hill,
Houghton, Trimdon Grange and Kelloe. Likewise there is a
record of Harry fixing a pump within a well at the Hendon
paper works in Sunderland and of him undertaking similar
work for the Sunderland and South Shields Water Company
at their Cleadon pumping station.

In the summer of 1877, a rather tragic diving accident
occurred at the waterworks at Dalton-le-Dale near Seaham.
On June 30 of that year an official from the works requested the

Hetton Colliery, Sunderland. As a diver Harry Watts was often employed in undertaking repairs at flooded collieries in eastern Durham.

service of Watts to remove a plug from a pilot shaft at the works and replace it with a new plug. On learning that the depth of the shaft was 25 fathoms (150 feet) Harry declined the work on the basis of his age.

Harry was by this time fifty-one years of age and although he was able to carry out normal duties as a diver within the comparatively shallow depths of the river, the pressure at these depths was potentially dangerous for a man of his age. Harry explained to the official that if a person's life were in danger he would willingly dive to such a depth, but would not risk his own safety for the purpose of maintenance. The waterworks official asked Harry where he might find a suitable diver for the job and Watts gave him a list of such men.

From Harry's list a diver called Mr. Littleboy from Tyne Dock was employed by the water company. Despite his name, this diver turned out to be a rather stout gentleman of eighteen stone. On the morning of July 5, 1877, Littleboy descended the shaft which was 10 feet in diameter. He was assisted by his brother and a cousin who attended an air pump above ground. It was a long descent just to reach the water. Once he was at work signals were sent down to Littleboy every quarter of an hour and on each occasion he would successfully respond until about 2pm when Littleboy failed to signal. This alerted those at the surface that Littleboy was very likely in danger and attempts were made to pull him up. They failed, because according to one later report, the air pipe had come into contact with the pump.

It had been a week since Harry had been approached by the water company to undertake the work so he was surprised to be paid a visit by an engineer of the RWC who came on behalf of the water company asking Harry for assistance.

Since the task could possibly result in the saving of someone's life Harry agreed to do the work. When Watts arrived at Dalton there were two divers from Seaham already at the scene but they seemed reluctant to make a descent, so Harry quickly changed into his diving gear.

The depth of the water in which Harry had to dive had been reduced by 30 feet, but 120 feet was still a considerable depth. Firstly, though Harry had to make an initial descent of 312 feet from the surface just to reach the level at which the water started. We should remember of course that the whole descent was shrouded in complete darkness.

So, down went Harry at 9pm that evening, trusting his life to his own experience as well as placing it in the hands of those working at the surface. Harry placed himself inside a basket called a kibble which was lowered via a winch at the shaft entrance in much the same manner as a bucket might be lowered into a well. It was by this means that he descended the first 312 feet, where, upon reaching the water level he signalled to the surface before entering the water into which he descended a further 120 feet, feeling his way down with his hands, using the air pipe and rope of Mr. Littleboy to guide him in the darkness.

As he dived to greater depths Harry had to carefully regulate and constantly adjust the valve in his helmet to keep the pressure within his suit in line with the ever changing pressure of water that surrounded him as he continued to descend. Any dizziness or even accompanying euphoria that he might experience, should he have made an error, would impair his judgment with potentially fatal results.

Eventually Harry reached the stage, or platform, on which Littleboy should have been working but after feeling his way down Littleboy's rope the fellow diver could not be found. Carefully and cautiously, working in pressures of 52lb, Harry knelt on the platform taking care not to lose his balance. Feeling along the rope in total darkness, Harry traced the rope beneath the stage.

A nineteenth century diving helmet

Sadly, it was then that Harry discovered beneath the staging, the feet of Mr. Littleboy who was suspended upside down. It is possible that Littleboy had fainted and fallen from the stage. This would have caused the air pressure to force the diver up against the stage, feet first. Unfortunately the escape valve in the diving helmet would have been ineffectual in this downward position and the air supply to Littleboy would have simply continued to fill his suit, inflating it like a rubber ball, rigidly stiffening the arms of his suit and rapidly exerting pressures which the human body could simply not have withstood. Harry was well aware by this time that Littleboy was dead and had been for several hours.

At around 9.15pm Harry returned to the surface and

delivered the sad news of Littleboy's death. Harry might have recovered Littleboy's body right there and then but had returned because he felt that his ribs were being broken by the pressure. At the time these were not depths that even an experienced diver could comfortably work in for more than a few minutes and Harry was past the age where it was safe for him to so. Despite this, Harry returned once again to the depths of the shaft and recovered the body of the unfortunate Mr. Littleboy. Harry would still not undertake the work of removing the plug that he had originally been asked to carry out and in the end the job was completed by a company from London.

A busy scene before 1929 showing the old Sunderland bridge prior to the construction of the present Wearmouth Brdge

The Giant Crab

BY MATTHEW BROWN
Grangetown Primary School, Sunderland

Grangetown Young Writers

G iant crab
I thought I would be dead
A nd I could be lying in bed
N ever seen so much anger
T errorising the sea

C rab ripping the suit on my thigh
R acing away like a steam train
A lthough he got away and to the surface he was in so
   much pain
B eing deadly ill he was in bed for 8 months because
   of the deadly crab.

Reward and Recognition

"*The chairman referred to the meeting as the most interesting one he had been called upon to attend since his election to the Mayoralty. The bravery possessed by Mr. Watts was of the highest order of bravery. He did not 'seek the bubble reputation at the cannon's mouth,' he was truly brave, and had rescued many a man from a watery grave. He had done brave deeds when there had been no applauding multitudes to see him, the only reward he got being a good conscience.*"

Sunderland Daily Echo, December 4th, 1878.

On October 17, 1866, something happened to Harry which had never happened before, he was recognised for his achievements. The first body to reward him was the Royal Humane Society, a charity established in 1774 as the Society for the Recovery of Persons Apparently Drowned to promote lifesaving efforts in the case of drowning. Established by William Hawes and Thomas Cogan on April 18, 1774 at the Chapter Coffee House in London, the Royal Humane Society's founders set out to educate people about new techniques for resuscitation.

The society quickly expanded, establishing "receiving houses" across the capital where the bodies of drowned people could be taken, so that those skilled in resuscitation techniques could attempt to restore them to life. These initial efforts expanded, in the coming years, to include recognising the bravery of people who had saved or attempted to save lives,

Trafalgar Square where Harry received a parchment from the Royal Humane Society

and it was in this capacity that they first became acquainted with Harry Watts.

At a Royal Humane Society meeting at their offices in Trafalgar Square, London, they agreed to present Harry with a parchment acknowledging his actions in saving William Hall from the Wear on September 5, 1866.

Although the Royal Humane Society was the first body to recognise Harry's achievements, the first to really celebrate him was quite a lot closer to home, the Diamond Swimming Club and Humane Society of Sunderland. In 1868 Harry was presented with the bronze medal of the Humane Society and a gold medal from the Diamond Swimming Club for the 25 lives he had saved to this point.

In August 1869 Harry received an Honorary Testimonial from the Royal Humane Society for saving the life of a shipwright named James Watt, Harry's twenty-sixth rescue, who had fallen into the South Dock Basin on July 21 that year. Harry had swam out to Watt and brought him to safety.

Victorian scene showing men at Sunderland harbour

Over the years, Harry continued to collect a number of different awards for his efforts. In 1875 he was given a large illustrated bible by the Brougham Street Sunday School. Later that year he was given a gold medal by a Mr Richardson for recovering his grandson's body from the Wear, one from the United Temperance Crusaders, and a gold watch from the Royal Humane Society. In 1877 he was given a silver medal by the sailors of the east end. He became something of a local celebrity, being regularly featured in the Sunderland newspapers, *The Echo* and *The Sunderland Times*.

The Echo itself had only been founded four years previously as *The Sunderland Daily Echo and Shipping Gazette*, to rival the two established weekly papers *The Sunderland Times* and *The Sunderland Herald*. Its championing of Harry brought him to new prominence and fame. By this time, due to his daring and bravery, Harry had collected a great number of medals. In August 1878 he lent them to the James Williams Street Christian Lay Church to exhibit at a bazaar they were holding, in the hope that seeing the medals would be a great attraction for the people of Sunderland.

During the night, the church was broken into, and Harry's medals were stolen. The theft incensed the people of the town, with an editorial in *The Sunderland Times* condemning the theft and calling for the medals to be replaced. The people of Sunderland responded wholeheartedly, forming a committee and donating to cover the cost of new medals.

The robber, a Mr John Bailey of 6 Grey Street, Southwick, was arrested for an unrelated burglary some time later, and in the course of his interrogation confessed to the theft of Harry's medals from the church. He'd given the medals to his eight year old daughter to play with, and when she'd grown tired of them she threw them into the fire.

On December 3, 1878, at a public meeting in the Christian Lay Church from which the medals had been stolen, the Mayor of Sunderland Samuel S. Robson presented Harry with

Harry Watts' medals would eventually be donated to Sunderland's museum

a duplicate set in honour of his life saving achievements.

The honours were not undeserved either. Between becoming a diver in 1861 and the public meeting to present the duplicate medals in 1878, Harry had rescued sixteen separate people from drowning, in addition to the seventeen people he had rescued before starting work for the River Wear Commissioners.

These rescues had not been without their dangers either. One particular rescue, reported in the local press, occurred on August 18 1875. Edward Bolton, a boy from Monkwearmouth, was playing near Pemberton's Drops. These were coal drops, positioned on the banks of the Wear to allow for the quick and easy loading of coal from Monkwearmouth Colliery onto ships on the river. Bolton was playing on the quayside by the drops when he fell into the river, and began to struggle. Fortunately, Harry was close by on one of the River Wear

Commissioners dredgers and, spotting Bolton in distress, dived in the water and swam to the boy's aid.

Twice Edward had sunk below the waves, and twice in his desperation he had managed to pull himself back to the surface, but as Harry reached him he was sinking under for a third time. When Harry got close, Edward, in his terror, gripped hold of Harry's legs and began to pull the pair of them under the water.

Beneath the surface of the water they went, Harry's life now in just as much danger as Edward's had been before Harry's intervention, and it took a gargantuan effort to pull them both to safety. It was not the first time that Harry had risked his life in a rescue, nor would it be the last, but his willingness to put his life on the line in order to save the life of complete strangers is a remarkable testament to the man's character.

The rescue of Edward Bolton was recognised by the Royal Humane Society, who in 1875 presented Harry with a certificate and a gold watch which had been paid for by the people of Sunderland.

A nineteenth century view of the river mouth in Sunderland

Heroism in the Watts family was not confined to Harry.

In 1877 Harry was working in the water near the South Pier, opposite the North Dock, clearing stones from the river. He was assisted by his son Tom, and a man called John Lonsdale, along with three other men. Harry was in the water, moving stones, when Tom looked up and saw a steamer leaving the North Dock. The steamer was behaving strangely, out of control, heading directly across the river towards the float with Tom and the other men aboard.

Tom immediately signalled to his father, and began hauling him out of the water. Just as Harry had made it onto the float the steamer struck, putting a hole in the side of the float which rapidly began to sink. Harry and the other men made it into a boat they had waiting nearby, and Tom was just about to join them when he noticed John Lonsdale coming out of the cabin of the float, and turned back to help him into the boat.

As he did so, the float sank, taking Lonsdale and Tom with it. Lonsdale, panicking in fear of his life, threw his arms around Tom's neck, the suction from the sinking float threatening to drown them both. Harry, still wearing the weighty diving gear, leapt into the bows of the boat just in time to catch hold of his son and haul the two men to safety.

During the 1880s there were two life-saving rescues credited to Harry Watts. The first involved the saving of a drowning lad called Jones in May 1881. Harry jumped into the Graving Dock, still wearing his diving gear and managed to bring the boy to safety, despite the hindrance of the suit. The second incident of the 80s occurred in August 1884 and was Harry's thirty-fifth life saving feat. A boy called James Riseborough fell into the outer basin of the River Wear and a large dog was sent to the rescue. Unfortunately the dog almost drowned the boy but Watts arrived at the scene just in time. Harry swam to the lad's rescue and brought him safely to shore. The fate of the dog is not recorded but it presumably found its way to safety.

The year 1884 was a year which saw a very narrow escape for Harry during one of his diving challenges. He was diving at the site of a freshly wrecked steamship called the *Adolphus* that was lying on its side. Enough of the ship was still above water for one of the ship's boilers to continue working. The boiler had continued to build up pressure and suddenly exploded. Workmen on the ship's poop deck were thrown everywhere and many were injured. One man would subsequently die from his injuries. Harry was lucky and despite the sudden shock, escaped without injury.

• • •

In 1887, three years after Sarah's death, Harry married for the third time. His new wife was Dorothy Jane Hunter, and was a widow with four children who were adopted by Harry. They lived together happily, by all accounts, until the end of Harry's life.

Harry's heroics continued throughout his life. Indeed, his last recorded rescue came at the age of 66. Harry and Dorothy were walking along the quayside towards their home on the South Dock when they heard a boy cry out as he fell into the water. Despite Dorothy's protestations, Harry went to see what had happened. When Dorothy saw the boy, who was called Fatherley struggling in the water, she is reported to have cried, "Be quick Harry, be quick!" as Harry leapt into the water, grabbed the boy, and swam to the edge of the dock where a rope was lowered.

In 1893, the year after this final rescue Harry sustained

an injury during a diving task that would severely affect his health. Throughout his lengthy and dangerous diving career, it is surprising that he had not suffered more injuries. On two

An elderly Harry Watts photographed with his medals

occasions he is known to have broken fingers and in another, an undated incident, he broke his leg after a ship's anchor fell onto his boat. He still managed to swim ashore and make his way to a doctor.

The injury of 1893 would prove to be more serious than this, affecting Harry's health in a way that he had not experienced since his treacherous dive into the soupy Thames at Wapping during his sailing days back in 1854. It was on a winter night in 1893 that some kind of problem with the dock gates at Sunderland's South Outlet had developed. Before the dive Harry seemed to have a premonition that something might go wrong. He instructed one of the assistants that if he should be delayed and his wife came to enquire about his whereabouts, the assistant should tell her that he would be no more than twenty minutes and that she should go and make supper.

Harry was sent down some twenty-five feet into the water to fix the problem. The darkness beneath was complete and he could only find his way around by touch. Somehow, Harry lost his signal rope and as he reached out to find it, his hand became jammed between a block and a chain that was being slowly hauled by a hydraulic machine. His fingers were trapped and he was unable to signal to the assistants above. Somehow he manoeuvred his entire body weight within his heavy diving costume onto his trapped hand and with an almighty wrench tore the hand away from the block ripping off part of one finger and causing injury to another.

He was bleeding heavily and on reaching the surface was taken to the infirmary. While he had been underwater Dorothy had come to enquire about the delay and followed the instructions given to her by the assistant. When she arrived home to make supper her instincts told her that something was seriously wrong and she prayed for Harry's life.

The exposure of the wounded finger to the murky waters would result in severe blood poisoning for Harry. The illness would last for eight months. "Aw wes black and blue fra th' croon o' me heed ti th' sole o' me fut" Harry later recalled. It would have been a very sad end if Harry's life had been taken in this way, but it was a measure of the love, recognition and respect that people held for Harry that visitors came from all over Britain to see him. One man even travelled from as far away as Toronto in Canada to see him.

During this period despite the seriousness of his illness Harry would regularly walk to Sunderland's Infirmary where he was an outpatient. Harry would recall that one doctor had recommended a glass of hot milk with a little rum in it to help his recovery, but Harry vehemently refused to take any rum even when the second opinion of another doctor backed up the suggestion. In the end when Harry did make a complete recovery without the help of alcohol Harry attributed the recoupment to prayer: "The Lord cured me," he said, " I lifted my hands ti' God an' prayed ti Him, an' I had prayin' people aboot me, an' He heard me, an' that's how I got cured,"

A river scene at Sunderland showing the new Wearmouth Bridge which was constructed in 1929

Harry's medals

BY ELEANOR BROOKE-TAYLOR
Grangetown Primary School, Sunderland

Grangetown Young Writers

Harry had a collection of medals which he had earned by diving in and saving people's lives. These medals were put in a display and this was how the thief found out about them.

When the thief stole the medals Harry was away, as the thief broke in he started to get a little nervous and shaky. As he tiptoed cautiously he heard creaking and started to sweat in case someone heard him. So he ran, grabbed the medals, and sped home, whilst worrying that someone had heard him.

When Harry got back he found that someone had broken in. Straight away he ran to find the most valuable things he had, his medals. Only to find that they were gone! As soon as he had thought about it he reported it to the police, he was totally shocked that someone could have actually been so horrible. Harry was absolutely devastated that they had gone. It was a tragedy that the only thing that he was proud of and that it was all ruined.

Tales of Tragedy

"We think the people of Sunderland may well feel satisfied at the assistance given by their townsman in the hope of recovering the bodies of the unfortunate victims, and to solve the mystery which at present surrounds the cause of the accident."

The Sunderland Weekly Times January 9, 1880.

For all the rewards Harry received in his life saving efforts there were many moments in Harry's life where his work proved to be a rather thankless and joyless task. Such work could range from the recovery of valuables for ungrateful captains to recovering the dead of those who had perished on days of tragedy.

There had been many, many occasions on which Harry had trawled the depths of the Wear searching on behalf of the relatives of lost loved ones who had last been seen near the river's edge. Sometimes the determined Harry would search endlessly until a body was found.

Such work prepared Harry for his part in the efforts that followed one of the worst disasters of the Victorian age. On January 1, of the year 1880 Harry headed north to Scotland in his capacity as a diver to assist in the recovery operation that followed the Tay Bridge disaster. Harry took with him his diving gear and two assistants, one of whom was a cousin and the other his son, Thomas. Also on board the train was a diver called Barclay from Shields with whom Harry would become momentarily entangled during his dive into the Tay.

The tragic event at the Tay Bridge had occurred during a violent storm on December 28, 1879. At around 7.15pm that day, a train thought to be carrying 75 people – both employees and passengers – was heading for Dundee on the north side of the Tay. It crossed the old Tay Bridge that spanned the two mile wide estuary but would never make it to the other side. The central girders of this bridge which had been built to inadequate specifications could not withstand the force of the storm that night. As the train attempted to cross, the central girders were blown into the river taking the steam locomotive and all of its carriages with it.

The recovery effort following the Tay Bridge disaster in January 1880

A steamer set out to search for survivors but no one was found. In the days that followed a call was put out for skilled divers to assist with the finding and recovery of bodies in the aftermath of this terrible event. Mr Dodds, the General Manager of the River Wear Commissioners heard the news of the disaster and in a discussion with the RWC Chairman, Sir James Laing he suggested that Harry Watts could be employed in helping the effort. Laing agreed and when Dodds approached Harry, he immediately agreed to assist with the work and offered his services free of charge.

One of Harry's first actions on arrival at Dundee was to buy himself a new knife as that often proved a useful tool in these operations. Harry found the waters of the Tay fast flowing and ridden with floating mud that made the visibility within the water very poor. On what seems to have been his first dive in the Tay he became entangled within telegraph wires that had fallen along with the bridge. This was a particular danger in the fast flowing tides of the river where Harry was surrounded by heavy wreckage from the train and the bridge that could have easily toppled in the current. Fortunately Harry's sharp new knife proved to be just the tool needed to cut him free from the wires, though he broke his little finger during the struggle.

Harry was in Scotland for a week though he was only diving at the site for three days. On one separate day during that week, he attended an enquiry along with other divers to give evidence about what they had found underwater. It was all part of the evidence-gathering effort to root out the causes of the accident. During his dives Harry explored the carriages of the train but found no bodies. On one dive he came across the steam locomotive but did not approach it fearing that there were too many things in which he could have become entangled. Remarkably, this locomotive was later recovered from the river and continued to serve as an active engine for many years to come.

There were huge girders from the bridge lying at the bottom of the river some of which encased the locomotive but despite the divers' searches no bodies were discovered. Most of those that were found were washed ashore or found "with drags". There were no survivors in the Tay Bridge disaster but in the end only 46 bodies were recovered, two of which were not found until February 1880. There were sixty known victims whose lives were claimed by this disaster and very probably several more that were never identified.

At 53 years of age Harry was the oldest and most experienced diver to assist with the recovery efforts in the Tay. Harry later recalled that on one morning a fellow diver offered a little

Divers prepare to work at the Tay Bridge disaster

something to keep him warm. "Cum an' ha' yer mornin' drappie", came the invitation from the Scottish diver. "What de ye mean?" asked Harry. When it was explained that he was being offered "a drap o' whisky, ti keep the caad oot", Harry launched straight into one of his temperance speeches:

> My man, aw'll tell tha what it is... aw'm twice as aad as ony on ye here, aw can wark as weel as ony on ye, an' if ye continee yer whisky drinkin' aw'll still be warkin' when ye're dune for.

What the fellow divers made of Harry's views on temperance is not recorded but his experience as a diver was certainly well-respected and acknowledged by the other men. "He seems to have gained the good opinions of all who witnessed the manner in which he went about his duties" reported *The Sunderland Weekly Times*.

The Edinburgh Evening News covering the story of the disaster also acknowledged the part that Watts played in the recovery effort and reported the following:

A diver descends into the River Tay during the Tay Bridge recovery operations in January 1880

Watts, who is evidently the most experienced diver of the lot, was complimented by Captain Brine, of the "Lord Warden," on the way he did his work. Watts was then on the ladder preparing for another descent, his son standing ready to screw on the mouthpiece, and replied 'That's all right. Thank ye kindly, sir.' Then with a 'Gan on, hinny,' to the man at the air pump, and Screw up !' to his son, he disappeared in an instant. He went in the direction of the engine, but the tide had now turned and was setting towards the girders, and he was obliged to give up. When his assistants had removed his ponderous dress it was found to be half filled with water. Watts has had an eventful career, and has saved thirty-three persons from drowning.

Though the recovery of dead bodies would not have been a pleasant aspect of work for a diver, Harry in speaking to *The Sunderland Weekly Times,* expressed his disappointment that the search had been brought to a sudden close. Harry's instinct was always to continue and not give up until bodies had been found. Despite the failure to find bodies the newspaper was full of praise for Harry's effort:

We think the people of Sunderland may well feel satisfied at the assistance given by their townsman in the hope of recovering the bodies of the unfortunate victims, and to solve the

A postcard commemorating the Tay Bridge disaster

mystery which at present surrounds the cause of the accident.

On January 8, 1880 Harry headed home to Sunderland.

* * *

Sadly, not everyone was so respectful of Harry's efforts as a diver. Back in Sunderland you might think it would come as something of a relief for Harry to be merely employed in the recovery of personal possessions. You would certainly expect this to be a far more pleasant, thankful and rewarding work than searching for bodies.

One such engagement took place during 1880 when Harry was requested to recover a purse belonging to the daughter of a sea captain who had fallen into a dock adjoining the River Wear. The captain's daughter had alighted from the ship at Sunderland's South Dock when she had slipped from the gangway into the water of the dock. She was quickly rescued, not by Watts on this occasion, but he soon became part of this story.

During her fall the young woman had lost a small leather bag containing £47, which was at that time, a rather significant sum. Attempts were made to recover the bag but they failed, so Harry Watts was called in to conduct the search in his capacity as a diver. Harry refused, on the grounds that it was a Sunday, but he agreed that he would attempt to recover the bag the following day. Monday came and Harry recovered the bag within minutes of diving. For his effort he was paid nothing more than the basic diver's fee in the presence of the captain and then only after the money in the bag had been counted, by the traffic manager of the RWC, presumably at the untrusting request of the captain.

A similar incident occurred involving a schooner called the *Susan* of Whitstable which sank at Sunderland's Ferry Boat Landing. Harry was employed in the raising of the vessel but before the vessel was raised the captain pleaded with Watts to recover £6 in gold from the schooner's state room along with a valuable watch, a chain, glasses and a ring. Harry agreed to this as the captain had claimed he was "very hard up". Risking his own life, Harry recovered the items but he had to break into the room underwater before conducting a very thorough search from which the items were eventually recovered. When the captain came the next day to collect the valuables he would not even thank Harry for his efforts.

It seemed that many people had come to expect Harry to carry out his heroics without any true appreciation of the skilled, dangerous and calm way that he undertook the work. This was perhaps exemplified by an incident a couple of years before the Tay Bridge disaster. On June 26, 1877 Alex

Mather of Arbroath, the master of a schooner called the *Hay and Catherine* was standing on board his ship at Wearmouth Drops on the River Wear. He stood close to a rope which came into contact with a passing steam tug called the *Bon Accord*.

Mather was caught by the rope and it dragged him to the ship's side mangling his leg and pulling off his foot completely leaving it hanging by only a piece of skin. Harry Watts and his son were working at the nearby Lambton Drops and heard the screams for help. They immediately came to Mather's rescue. Harry and his son jumped into a boat, unravelled Mather's leg from the rope and gave him first aid. They hailed a tug to get him to shore, and then a cab to take him to the infirmary.

All of the efforts to get Mather safely to hospital were no doubt performed in the cool, calm and collected way for which Harry had come to be noted. Not only that but once Mather had recovered from his ordeal, after months in hospital, Harry persuaded some Scottish captains to raise a subscription for Mather's welfare. This incident is not included amongst Harry's life saving acts but it is hard to imagine what might have became of Mather had he been left to hang for longer or had not been fortunate enough to find the capable assistance of Watts and his son so ready at hand.

Later, Mather composed a letter to *The Sunderland Daily Echo* from his home in Scotland in which he praised, at length, the work of the nurses at Sunderland's infirmary where his leg had been amputated, but he only gives a passing thanks to Harry Watts and his son. It is possible of course that Mather was mindful of Harry's modesty in his rescue work and did not wish to embarrass him.

Before we come to the saddest tragedy in which Harry Watts was employed, we should make mention of a tragic, but rather curious incident in the later years of his life in 1895 when Harry was 68 years of age. The incident occurred on January 19 of that year, as a ship from Hamburg called the *Erato* was berthed in Sunderland's South Dock. At around midday a nineteen year old lad called Kanscheit was sent into the forepeak of the vessel to collect a shovel. After a quarter of an hour he did not return so an officer descended into the same forepeak by ladder to seek him out. As he did so he was overcome with an overwhelming dizziness which rendered him helpless. A second officer who came to his assistance was likewise overcome. Fortunately they were hauled out by fellow seamen and in a state of trance they managed to indicate by gesturing, that Kanscheit was still below. The two men then collapsed on the deck.

Some of the seamen attended to the two men while two others descended the ladder only to succumb to the same symptoms as the two officers. Similarly rescued, they too were brought to the deck and likewise collapsed and the same process – a little bewilderingly perhaps - seems to have been followed again. A large crowd gathered, doctors attended and the inflicted were sent to the infirmary.

With Kanscheit still below it was not long before someone suggested that a diver might be employed in the search for the young lad. Harry Watts was soon on the scene and donning his full diving kit descended the ladder in search of Kanscheit. At first Harry could find nothing within the first floor of the forepeak. Searching deeper in the lower level of the forepeak he found that some of the fumes were finding their way into his diving suit. Harry started to feel the effects of mild dizziness and returned to the deck to take in some fresh air and drink a glass of water before continuing his search. This time Harry discovered the dead body of the young man in the lower level with a gash in his head having seemingly fallen, perhaps overcome with dizziness on the upper floor. Sadly another of the men who had attempted to search for the lad would die in the infirmary a few hours after he was admitted there. A coroner later attributed the causes of death on both counts to asphyxiation, resulting from the fumes released by a cask of black paint that had somehow become ignited.

* * *

Despite Harry's rewards, rescues, fame and longevity, tragedy and ill fortune often paid Harry a visit throughout his life. He had lost his mother and his father in his childhood and his brother had been lost to the sea. His first wife had died after she had succumbed to the perils of the North Sea and even his mother-in-law (through his second wife) had been lost, presumed drowned. Two of Harry's nephews were drowned from a steam boat on the North Sea and a cousin called Captain Crozier had drowned along with a daughter who he had taken away to better climes for the improvement of her health.

All of these events must have affected Harry personally and perhaps collectively contributed to his determination and instinct for saving lives. Nothing, however could have prepared anyone, including Harry, for the tragedy that would come to Sunderland on June 16, 1883. It was a tragedy that would claim the lives of the eight year old daughter and ten year old son of Harry's niece but these were only two of many lives taken that day in one of the saddest events in Britain's history. It was a catastrophe that touched the hearts of the world.

This tale of tragedy took place not in the depths of the sea or in the River Wear but on dry land in a theatre set against the serene and tranquil surroundings of Sunderland's Mowbray Park in the centre of the town on a summer afternoon.

In the week leading up to the tragedy, a leaflet was posted through the doors of many Sunderland residents. It was designed to attract the attention of children, particularly those from poor backgrounds for whom there was perhaps little joy and excitement in life. Distributed by a family of entertainers called the Fays of Tynemouth, the leaflet publicised a forthcoming "grand day performance for children" at the Victoria Hall Theatre in Toward Road on the fringe of Mowbray Park.

With promises of conjuring, talking waxworks, living marionettes and a grand ghost illusion all on offer for the entrance fee of one penny it captured the excitement of little minds throughout the town. For many though, perhaps the most exciting thing of all was the announcement that "every child entering the room will stand a chance of receiving a handsome present, books, toys &c"

Such was the excitement, that on the Saturday afternoon of

The Victoria Hall theatre and Mowbray Park before its destruction

The Victoria Hall was destroyed by a German bomb during the Second World War

June 16, 1883 some 2,000 children crowded into the theatre to see the show. The two-tiered theatre has long since gone, destroyed in 1941 by a German parachute bomb during the Second World War, but on that sad afternoon in 1883 it was a busy venue packed to the rafters with some 2,000 excited children. The performance began at 3pm and everything seems to have gone to plan. By 5.10pm the show was almost over. It was then the tragedy began.

Toys were thrown by the performers to the children nearest the stage causing an eruption of ever increasing excitement. This excitement spread quickly to the children in the upper gallery of the theatre who feared that they were out of reach and would miss out on the free flowing prizes. Many of the children in the gallery, mostly unaccompanied, made a rush for the narrow stairs heading towards the lower levels of the theatre. As they did so, more and more children were caught up in the euphoria that would follow.

The children continued to pour down the narrow stairway at the bottom of which was a slightly opened door. It opened inwards, but was bolted in place. Children were squeezed against the door and were unable to open it as more and more children joined the back of the queue and continued to push, unaware of the crush at the front.

It was the severe crushing in this narrow stairway, coupled with trampling amidst the panic and confusion that claimed the lives that day. The tragedy ended the lives of a staggering 183 Sunderland children. Of the deaths, around seventy of the children were seven or eight years old. Another sixty were aged from nine to eleven. The youngest fatalities were two girls aged three years old and the oldest, a girl of fourteen. In total 114 boys and 69 girls died.

Over twenty families lost more than one child that day and one family lost four children. As news of the event spread around the town crowds gathered outside the building, men

Distraught parents identify the bodies of their children following the Victoria Hall disaster

The Victoria Hall memorial in Sunderland's Mowbray Park

entered the building in the hope of finding their loved ones alive and all around there was wailing and hysteria.

It was an event that called for calm and experience and foremost amongst the helpers that day was Harry Watts. It is a mark of this man that Harry's involvement in the immediate aftermath of that tragedy should be singled out on such a terrible day where so many individual tragedies occurred, but Harry did receive a special mention for his role.

Speaking of the recovery effort one local newspaper reported:

one man worked splendidly and too much praise cannot be given to him. I think it was Mr. Watts. When others were excited and did nothing but wring their hands and cry out, he was cool and collected and rendered immense assistance.

At a meeting of Methodists held just after the disaster and attended by the Mayor of Sunderland the Mayor would also single out Harry for the role he played on that sad day:

I want to pay a tribute to one of your own members, I refer to my friend Henry Watts. I saw him lay hold of those little corpses one by one and move them with as soft a hand as a mother would. I do not hesitate to say here that he is a hero.

It would be too sad to recall all the names of those that lost their lives that day, but they hailed from streets across almost every part of the town from High Street West and High Street East to Brougham Street and Hendon Street. One of the dead was an eight year old Abraham Simey of Silver Street, the very street where Harry had been born. One family, the Mills family of Ann Street lost two daughters, Alice aged 10 and Elizabeth aged 12 along with two sons Richard aged 6 and Frederick aged 9. In Burleigh Street another family mourned the loss of William Henry Pescod aged 10 and Mary Eleanor Pescod aged 10. These were the two children of Harry's niece.

Illustrations in the Graphic depicting the Victoria Hall in June 1883

One of the toys given away to the children at the Victoria Hall

The news of the Victoria Hall disaster was quickly relayed around the world with reports in newspapers such as *The New York Times* moving people to tears. Some £5,000 was raised for the support fund including a rather modest contribution of £50 from Queen Victoria. The money was used to pay for funerals and for the memorial that can still be seen today in Mowbray Park close to the site where the Victoria Hall had once stood.

Sunderland's saddest day

BY NIAMH ALDERSON
Grangetown Primary School, Sunderland

Grangetown Young Writers

On a Wednesday in June 1883 all the poor children in Sunderland got a letter through their door saying "The greatest day of your child's life. On Saturday afternoon at 3 o'clock all children can come to the Victoria Hall and get a little toy each."

On Saturday June 16, 1884, more than 2000 children gathered in the Victoria Hall. There was puppetry, magic, and ventriloquism. Then the man started to throw the small toys to the bottom of the theatre. The children at the top started to worry that they would miss out, so they all ran down the stairs and came to a door which they thought opened outwards but which actually opened inwards. They all got squashed and couldn't breathe properly. After that the law was changed so that the doors were always to open outwards. 183 people died, 114 boys and 64 girls, over twenty families lost children, one family lost four children.

When the news reached the nation people saved up and they got £5,000. This paid for funerals and for the memorial which stands in Mowbray Park. The news shocked the world. It was Sunderland's saddest day.

Harry Watts was very calm about this, and helped to get the bodies out of the Victoria Hall, even though all of the other people were crying. Two of the children who died were Harry's Niece's children. They were called Mary and William Pescod.

A Lifesaving Legacy

"In writing the final words of this imperfect story of the life and labours of Harry Watts, I feel that I cannot do better than liken him to one of those fine old ships. Like them he bears the scars of a long and honourable service; and though now, in his 85th year, he is, like them, laid by in harbour as "Past Active Service," there is still that about him which commands our respect, still that dignity of bearing which only such service can bring; and a history which may well inspire the younger generation to emulate his heroic deeds. "

Alfred Spencer, *Life of Harry Watts* 1911.

From around 1850, and his return from sea to married life with Rebecca, Harry Watts had been an important member of Sunderland's life boat service. Records show that Harry had a part in saving the lives of at least 120 people in his service for the lifeboat. This was in addition to the 36 lives he had saved in his own time by individual effort.

Sunderland's lifeboat station is the oldest in the country, first being founded in 1800. Twenty-four years before the foundation of the RNLI, the people of Sunderland had recognised the importance of organising a lifeboat, paid for by the sailors and ship owners of Sunderland. Although taken over by the RNLI in 1865, Sunderland has had lifeboats in constant operation since that first foundation, occupying twelve different sites at different points around the port.

Harry Watts was not the only famous Sunderland hero to hold a position in the lifeboat crew. Indeed, in 1856, a silver medal was awarded to Joseph Hodgson for his efforts over the previous 12 years, during which he had saved 10 people from drowning, and a further 17 as part of the lifeboat crew. Hodgson was something of a celebrity in Sunderland at the time, much like Harry would go on to become, and was known by the nickname, "The Stormy Petrel".

Harry Watts and Joseph Hodgson had a great deal in common. Hodgson was born in Dunning Street, Bishopwearmouth in 1829, three years after Harry, and by the age of 10 his formal education at Gray's School in Sunderland was over. He started work as part of a gang of riggers. Hodgson showed a talent for art, becoming a painter at 12 years of age.

Hodgson's first rescue came aged 15, when he leapt to the rescue of a three year old who had fallen into the River Wear.

That same year he rescued John Nicholson, and in 1847 he saved John Marshall, a local carver, from drowning in the river near to the Ferry Boat Landing. Hodgson discovered he was colourblind, and in gratitude for saving his life Marshall trained him as a carver and a decorator.

Hodgson continued his life-saving work, receiving a gold medal from Emperor Napoleon III of France for his January 1857 rescue of the crew of *Les Trois Soeurs*, a French ship wrecked off the coast of Sunderland. He and Harry worked closely together as part of the lifeboat crew, indeed Harry is said to have enjoyed telling a story about Hodgson. Hodgson wanted to try his hand at diving, so Harry agreed to lend him his equipment. Unfortunately, the collar piece of Harry's diving suit was too small to fit over Hodgson's head. Keeping a totally straight face, Harry sent a workman for an axe, claiming he would remedy the problem by cutting off Hodgson's nose.

A lifeboat on the north east coast

Joseph Hodgson remained an important part of the Sunderland lifeboat crew until 1869, when he moved to London to take up a job working for the West African Shipping Company. He was given further medals from the Mayor of Sunderland in 1883, and the Humane Society, and saved the life of an interpreter on a voyage to Africa. Unfortunately, Hodgson fell on hard times towards the end of his life, being forced to pawn his medals and ending his life in a slum in Poplar, east London. Joseph Hodgson, "The Stormy Petrel", died on October 15, 1908, aged 79. He is buried in East London Cemetery in Newham.

"The Stormy Petrel" may have gone to London, but Harry Watts remained in Sunderland, and remained part of the lifeboat crew. So respected was he that he was voted a Honorary Life Member of the Volunteer Life Brigade, one of only two recorded in the society's rolls in 1909-10.

The dangers of the lifeboat were not limited to the sea. On one occasion, when the Italian barque *Julia Ravenna* wrecked off the coast of Sunderland, Harry and the lifeboat were dispatched to rescue the crew. No sooner had they been transported safely to land that the ship started to break up. Several members of the Italian crew tried to get back on board the *Julia Ravenna*, including one who rushed Harry and kicked him in the stomach, seriously injuring him and leaving him coughing up blood. Such was the spirit among the lifeboat crew, however, that such an assault on Harry did not go unpunished, as a fight broke out between the Italians and local men who were spectators at the event.

Devoted as he was in his service however, only a piece of great good fortune prevented Harry Watts from ending his life in poverty, just as Joseph Hodgson had. Harry retired from his job with the River Wear Commissioners at the age of 70, after thirty years service. The River Wear Commissioners did not give pensions, and although they were willing to put Harry into a nominal job so that he could continue to be supported, Harry turned their offer down. He had saved diligently, and invested his money, and he believed that his investments would be sufficient to see him through his old age.

Unfortunately for Harry, his investments did not turn out to be as profitable as he would have hoped, and it was not long before he found himself in difficult circumstances.

Fortunately for Harry, on October 21, 1909, the Scottish-born American steel magnate and philanthropist Andrew Carnegie came to Sunderland.

Andrew Carnegie

Carnegie had been born in Dunfermline, and emigrated to the United States as a child, starting work in a cotton mill at the age of 13. He did several different jobs, from bobbin boy at the cotton mill to messenger for the Ohio Telegraph Company, then a telegraph operator for the Pennsylvania Railroad Company. His time at the Pennsylvania Railroad Company gave him valuable management experience and put him in touch with influential members of the burgeoning American business community.

Carnegie's investments in the railways continued to grow, and he reinvested the money in other areas including, notably, iron and steel production. It was to be the steel industry which made Carnegie's fortune, with numerous steel mills across the Eastern United States. By 1889, due in no small part to the efforts of Carnegie, the United States was producing more steel than the United Kingdom. It made Carnegie a very rich man, one of the wealthiest in the world, and when he formed the United States Steel Corporation in 1901 he created the world's first billion dollar company.

Whilst being an incredibly successful businessman, Carnegie was also a committed philanthropist. In 1883 he began a campaign of library building. Carnegie Libraries, as they became known, would spread across the globe, with 2,509 being built between 1883 and 1929. The first was built in Carnegie's hometown of Dunfermline, with others constructed in the United Kingdom, United States, Canada, Australia, New Zealand, Serbia, Mauritius, Fiji and the Caribbean. Sunderland was possessed of three, and it was for the grand opening of the third that Carnegie visited Sunderland in 1909.

As well as the Carnegie Libraries, in 1904 Carnegie had established the Carnegie Hero Fund, following a mining disaster in Pittsburgh, Pennsylvania. 181 men died in the disaster at Hardwick Colliery, including two who had given their lives in rescue attempts. On hearing of the disaster, Carnegie donated $50,000 to the relief fund, doubling the amount raised by public subscription. The Hero Fund's purpose was to recognise those who had taken heroic measures to save human life and to support them or their families.

Before Carnegie's visit to Sunderland, Mr J. G. Addison, who had donated the site for the Monkwearmouth Library, wrote to the public librarian asking for the records of Harry's heroism. Addison felt that Harry was exactly the kind of person the Hero Fund had been established to help. Carnegie, upon hearing of Harry's actions, and of his difficult financial circumstances, said:

He shall never want again in this world. He has evidently been a brave man. It is fine to come across a man who is not only a physical but a moral hero.

Carnegie met Harry that evening, the two talking for so long that the meeting to grant Carnegie the Freedom of the

Monkwearmouth Library

Borough was delayed. In his speech at the dinner, Carnegie gave the quote with which this book began:

> *I have today been introduced to a man who has, I think, the most ideal character of any man living on the face of the earth. I have shaken hands with a man who has saved thirty-six lives. Among the distinguished men whose names the Mayor has recited, you should never let the memory of this Sunderland man die. Compared with his acts, military glory sinks into nothing. The hero who kills men is the hero of barbarism; the hero of civilisation saves the lives of his fellows.*

Leaving Sunderland, Carnegie ensured that Harry, "the bravest man I have ever met", was granted 25 shillings a week for the rest of his life, with the pension to pass to his wife if she outlived him. Harry's financial problems were immediately solved, and he lived out the rest of his life in relative comfort.

The lasting legacy of Harry's life was not just in the lives he saved. In around 1885, whilst working for the River Wear Commissioners, Harry discovered a canoe, buried in the Wear at Hylton. When Harry discovered it, experts believed it to be prehistoric in origin. Recently experts have reassessed its age, and it is now thought to be medieval. The canoe itself was donated to Sunderland Museum, where it retains pride of place, alongside Harry's medals.

This historic canoe, discovered by Harry Watts around 1885, can still be seen in Sunderland's museum

Although Harry's heroics were never recognised with a statue, in 1910 the Mayor and other notable gentlemen of Sunderland commissioned Alfred Spencer, the editor of *The Sunderland Echo*, to write a book about Harry's life. Spencer's book, *Life of Harry Watts; Sixty Years Sailor & Diver*, was published the following year. Before becoming editor of *The Echo*, Spencer had worked as a life insurance agent, and as traffic manager at an ironworks. Born in Bermondsey, he died on February 12, 1913, at the age of 63.

Harry Watts passed away just over two months later, on April 23. During his 86 years he had seen the reign of King George IV, Queen Victoria, Edward VII and George V. He had seen the British Raj established in India, as Britain became the most powerful nation on the planet. He had seen the move from sailing ships to steam ships, and the establishment of professional football. He had lived through the reform of the Poor Laws, the repeal of the Corn Laws, and the introduction of laws which vastly increased the number of people eligible to vote.

Sunderland, in particular, had changed an awful lot over Harry's lifetime. Over the preceding 86 years it had become one of the most important and prosperous shipbuilding towns in the country. The Borough of Sunderland had been created in 1835, with Sunderland and Bishopwearmouth becoming one town, Monkwearmouth too being absorbed in 1897.

Although the wars, and the decline in heavy industry and coalmining, were to take their toll on Sunderland during the twentieth century, at the time of Harry's death the town was at a peak. 1906 had been the best year in Sunderland's history for shipbuilding, with 91 ships launched on the Wear, coal mining, rope making, glass making and the pottery industries continued to thrive, and Sunderland's prosperity led to the growth and development of the town, with key civic buildings like the Empire Theatre opening in 1907, and the Queen Alexandra Bridge, the heaviest bridge in the country at the time, opening in 1909.

Harry himself had saved 36 people from drowning, fathered nine children and adopted another four, served as a merchant seaman, a diver, participated in the rescue of 120 people as part of Sunderland's lifeboat crew, been recognised by his peers and rewarded by Andrew Carnegie. He had seen Sunderland change beyond all recognition, had a book written to tell his life story, and had earned numerous medals and awards.

Remembering Harry

"*If I walk by the River Wear tomorrow and see someone struggling in the water, where do I turn to decide what to do? The answer is history. What would Harry Watts have done? History provides role models and prompts the great question, 'Who am I?'*"

Terry Deary, *The Daily Telegraph*, September 2012.

In a quiet quarter of Sunderland's Grangetown Cemetery lies a one hundred year old grave. Weathered and forgotten its inscription is worn and indecipherable. It is the grave of Harry Watts, an unremarkable slab of stone. It is a poor epitaph for a remarkable life but at the time of writing it is the nearest thing to a memorial for Harry.

How an extraordinary man like Harry came to be so widely forgotten, even in his hometown, is a matter of debate. Harry's modest ways and humble origins could have been factors but it may be significant that a little over a year after his death, Britain and much of Europe was plunged into the darkness of the First World War. The death and sacrifice, the acts of heroism and bravery that accompanied the Great War soon overshadowed the lives and events of earlier times.

Given time, Harry's story might have grown in stature. Who knows, perhaps it could have achieved the status of a local legend in the years that followed his death. Sadly, this was not to be. It seems the popular memory of Harry's incredible story was yet another forgotten victim of the war.

If it were not for Alfred Spencer or the medals at Sunderland Museum, Harry would not be remembered at all. In later years, those who came to know of Harry's life, through Spencer's work, could see that here was a man who deserved to be remembered, a man whose selfless acts of bravery were an example to us all but it seemed the time had passed for remembering Harry.

This would change in 2012. As the one hundredth anniversary of Harry's death approached, a new opportunity arose to remember Harry's profile and bring his story to public attention once again. Here was the chance to finally give Harry the lasting recognition he deserved.

During that year, the Sunderland-born writer Terry Deary would put his weight behind a campaign to remember our hero. Harry's story had first come to the attention of Terry in 2011 and through his local contacts and media connections he was determined to raise the profile of Harry Watts.

Writing in *The Daily Telegraph* in September 2012, Terry remarked:

At the moment I'm looking into the story of a man called Harry Watts from Sunderland — a forgotten hero who died 100 years ago. Last winter, a fire service crew refused to wade into an icy lake to reach a man because health and safety rules said that they shouldn't if the water came over their knees.

Terry went on to describe how Harry had rescued many people from drowning by:

...jumping into cold and filthy rivers around the world. If I walk by the River Wear tomorrow and see someone struggling in the water, where do I turn to decide what to do? The answer is history. What would Harry Watts have done? History provides role models and prompts the great question, "Who am I?"

By November 2012, Terry Deary's campaign to commemorate Watts had gained significant momentum. "Help remember our forgotten hero" proclaimed a headline in *The Sunderland Echo* outlining the mission to make Harry Watts famous. There was mention of Andrew Carnegie's wish that Watts should never be forgotten. Terry believed that was exactly what had happened and he wanted to change that. Though Deary is not a proponent of a statue to Watts' memory, as that would be an expensive gesture in times of austerity there was a feeling there should be something. "We would all benefit from remembering Harry's courage" stated Terry.

Earlier that month Terry had hosted a TV documentary for BBC's *Inside Out* in which he highlighted Harry's remarkable life and the plans to commemorate him. In the programme Terry interviewed representatives of Sunderland City Council, Sunderland Museum, a Sunderland heritage group and the local publishing company, My World and it was generally agreed that Harry Watts was a man who deserved to be remembered.

Through Terry's energy and gift of persuasion several activities and events were organised in 2013 to remember Harry. They included the launch of this book *Harry Watts, The Forgotten Hero* and the introduction of some permanent memorials to Harry's name. At Sunderland Museum and Winter Gardens an event was organised for the hundredth anniversary of Harry's death on April 23, where a room was renamed in Harry's honour along with a new exhibition remembering his life.

At Sunderland's Empire Theatre, a seat with a plaque recalls Harry's name and there are plans to introduce a blue plaque in Sunderland to remember Harry, though the location for this particular memorial has yet to be decided. Elsewhere, efforts are being made to trace Harry's descendants with a view to installing a commemorative plaque at Harry's grave.

Undoubtedly one of the most pleasing aspects in commemorating Harry in 2013 has been the involvement of young people, not just those who have contributed to this book, but also those involved in a wide range of activities organised to recall his life.

A generation or two may have forgotten the story of Harry Watts but hopefully that will now change. It seems fitting that Harry, who saved the lives of so many young people, should be remembered by the younger generation who can learn so much from Harry's life and times.

Harry Watts, it seems will no longer be the forgotten hero, may he be remembered for many generations to come.

Harry's Lifesaving Rescues

1. Saves fellow apprentice Richard Nicholson at Quebec, in 1839. Nicholson fell overboard and Watts jumped in to rescue him.

2. At Miramichi in New Bruunswick Harry rescued Captain Luckley from a capsized a canoe in 1839. Watts had been waiting for him at the gangway .

3. While coming through the Pentland Firth in Scotland on board a brig called the *United Kingdom* in around 1843 a lad called George Watson was washed overboard, Watts came to his rescue and returned him to the ship.

4 and 5. In 1845, on board the Protector at Woolwich Watts saved two men on board a sinking barge.

6 to 11. At Rotterdam in 1847 Watts saved six men whose boat was smashed by a falling anchor.

12. In 1852 a boy named Paul was saved from drowning near Sunderland's South Pier. Harry jumped in and saved him, though they boy's mother showed no appreciation for Harry's efforts.

13. In 1852 Watts rescued a boy named Matthew Maughan from the River Wear near Smurthwaite's Wharf.

14. Watts rescued a young woman in 1853. She was attempting to commit suicide in the sea near the pier at the mouth of the river.

15. A girl was saved by Harry after she had fallen into the canal at Cardiff in 1853.

16. Watts rescued William Smith, a trimmer, who had fallen into a dock adjoining the River Wear in 1853.

17. Harry saved saved a boy at Wapping Dock in 1854. This resulted in a serious illness that lasted three months, due to swallowing poisonous water.

18 and 19. Harry rescued two boys from a boat that capsized in severe weather near Sunderland's South Outlet in 1862

20 and 21. A girl and a boy were rescued by Harry after falling from the quay near Sunderland's Panns Ferry in 1863.

22. In 1866 Watts rescued a boy named Smith who fell from a dredger at the number 2 Graving Dock.

23. In September 1866 Watts rescued a boy named Hall who fell overboard near the River Wear Commissioners' Quay.

24. Also in 1866 a boy fell from the Custom House Quay and was brought ashore by Watts.

25. A boy called John Fox fell from a boat at the Mark Quay. Watts saved him.

26. In July, 1869 Watts rescued a shipwright called James Watt who had fallen into the South Dock basin.

27. Watts rescued at least one of a party of eight children in June, 1870 who were on board a pleasure boat which capsized in the River Wear. In truth Watts was probably responsible for rescuing the majority of the party.

28. On that very same day in June 1870 Watts had to jump into the river again, this time to save his colleague, Robert Wilson.

29. Later in 1870 Watts rescued a boy who had fallen into the Wear near the Tide Gauge Jetty.

30. In August, 1875 Watts saved a boy called Edward Bolton and was nearly drowned owing to the boy clutching him round the legs.

31. Watts rescued a boy named James Taylor in September 1876. He had fallen into the river near Mark Quay.

32. A boy named Henry Dobson, fell into the river in November 1876 and was rescued by Watts

33. A man named John Lonsdale was rescued by Harry Watts after he was dragged overboard from a keel by a heavy chain in May, 1877.

34. In May, 1881 Harry rescued a lad named Jones from the Graving Dock.

35. Watts rescued a boy named James Riseborough from the outer basin in August, 1884, after a big dog had failed to help him.

36. In May 1892 a boy named Fatherley was rescued from the South Dock. The rescue took place in the presence of Harry's wife.

About the Authors

David Simpson is a former journalist and an author of over thirty books on British history, topography and culture. He has published titles on London and Scotland as well as publications featuring British nostalgia, history and popular tastes from the 1940s to the 1990s. His special interest is North East history and dialect and he has entertained and lectured widely on the subject. David has appeared in over a hundred television and radio broadcasts both locally and nationally.

Richard Callaghan was born in Durham City and educated at Birmingham and Glasgow Universities. He is the author of over twenty books. He has written both for adults and for a family audience on a whole host of subjects including both global and local history. Richard is co-author of *My Sunderland*, *My Scotland* and *My London* as well as the My Year series of books featuring events, culture and current affairs from the 1940s to the late 1990s.

For more details visit **www.myworld.co.uk**